The Rushdie Letters

THE
Rushdie
Letters

Freedom to Speak,
Freedom to Write

Edited by Steve MacDonogh
in association with
Article 19

University of Nebraska Press

LINCOLN

First published in 1993 in Great Britain
and Ireland by Brandon Book Publishers Ltd
Dingle, Co. Kerry, Ireland

Published simultaneously in the United States
by the University of Nebraska Press

Library of Congress Cataloging in Publication Data
The Rushdie letters : freedom to speak,
freedom to write /
edited by Steve MacDonogh in association
with Article 19.
p. cm.   (Stages series)   ISBN 0-8032-3174-1 (hard)
ISBN 0-8032-8198-6 (pbk.)
1. Rushdie, Salman. Satanic verses. 2. Freedom of the
press – History – 20th century. 3. Islam and literature –
History – 20th century. 4. Authors – 20th century –
Correspondence. 5. Censorship – History – 20th
century. 6. Freedom of speech in Islam.
I. MacDonogh, Steve. II. Article 19 (Organization).
III. Series.
PR6068.U757S27364 1993 823′ .914–dc20
92-46585 CIP

This book is published with
the financial assistance of The Arts Council/
An Chomhairle Ealaíon, Ireland

Typeset by Brandon

Manufactured in the United States
of America

Everyone has the right of freedom of opinion and expression; this right includes freedom to hold opinions without interference and to seek, receive and impart information and ideas through any media and regardless of frontiers.

Article 19 of the Universal Declaration of Human Rights

Contents

Introduction / 9

SALMAN RUSHDIE: ONE THOUSAND DAYS

IN A BALLOON / 13

LETTERS TO SALMAN RUSHDIE / 25

Günter Grass / 27

Paul Theroux / 31

Arnold Wesker / 35

Margaret Atwood / 39

Nadine Gordimer / 43

Jatinder Verma / 47

Peter Carey / 51

Fahimeh Farsaie / 55

José Saramago / 59

Graham Swift / 63

William Styron / 65

Dermot Bolger / 69

Norman Mailer / 73

Elfriede Jelinek / 75

Kazuo Ishiguro / 79

Johannes Mario Simmel / 81

Ralph Giordano / 87

Pierre Guyotat / 91

Avraham B. Yehoshua / 93

Mario Vargas Llosa / 95

Andrzej Szczypiorski / 99

Gertrud Seehaus / 103

Dragan Velikic / 107

Joachim Walther / 111

Lev Kopalev / 115

Tom Stoppard: On the third anniversary

of the *fatwa* / 117

Salman Rushdie: Reply / 121

CARMEL BEDFORD: FICTION, FACT AND THE *FATWA* / 125

About the authors / 184

Introduction

The Rushdie Letters represents the culmination of an international campaign by writers and others in solidarity with Salman Rushdie and his publishers. In February 1992, after three years of sustained campaigning by the International Committee for the Defence of Salman Rushdie and his Publishers (ICDSR), the German newspaper *die tageszeitung* led a consortium of newspapers in publishing a series of letters from eminent writers to the author. These letters, by writers representing a wide range of opinion, were taken up by newspapers in Argentina, Austria, Belgium, Brazil, Canada, Denmark, France, Greece, Hungary, Ireland, Israel, Italy, Norway, Portugal, Russia, Spain, Sweden, Switzerland, the United Kingdom, the United States and Yugoslavia.

"Fiction, Fact and the *Fatwa*", the chronology of events surrounding the publication of the novel and declaration of the *fatwa*, is a record of outrage – expressed by two opposing sides, and in very different ways. It illustrates sad and shocking deviations from the principle of the right to free expression, the consequences of which have been disastrous to many and to one man in particular.

The consequences for the democratic process are equally depressing. Essentially, the case of *The Satanic Verses* is reduced to one simple and terrifyingly clear choice: is the principle of freedom of expression to be held to ransom now and in the future by groups who have been offended by the words of a writer, or will there be firm action to defend and insist upon this fundamental tenet of democracy?

Many thousands of words have been written on both sides; argument about the right to freedom of expression has, over a period of almost four years, become blurred. Many of those governments who, when the *fatwa* was first pronounced in February 1989, strongly upheld the principle of the right to expression, have slowly, but inexorably, changed their position, not always in words, but tellingly in actions.

On the day following the pronouncement of the *fatwa,* the European Community issued a resolution demanding that the *fatwa* be rescinded; the UK government expressed its dismay in the strongest possible terms stating that Iran had failed to respect international standards. On 20 February 1989, European Community governments issued a joint declaration and recalled their ambassadors from Tehran. The Canadian government spoke of the *fatwa* as a fundamental breach of international law and practice, and the following day the US government decided to postpone indefinitely any possibility of normalized trade or diplomatic relations with Iran.

By 3 March, however, the UK Prime Minister Margaret Thatcher and Foreign Secretary Sir Geoffrey Howe had conceded that *The Satanic Verses* was offensive to Muslims, and by 22 March the European Community had issued a decision to allow member countries to return their ambassadors to Iran. The British government on 27 September 1990 renewed diplomatic relations with Iran on the understanding that Iran would respect international law.

On 8 September 1990, an article by former UK Conservative Party Chairman Norman Tebbit in the *Independent* marked a shocking stage in the 1,000 days of the *fatwa,* because the premise on which the case previously rested shifted fundamentally. It appeared from that day on that the issue was no longer the right to freedom of expression, but whether or not an individual has the right *credentials* to be allowed to speak his opinions. According to Norman Tebbit, Salman Rushdie owed respect and gratitude to the British public for accepting him as a foreigner, and that by writing *The Satanic Verses* and offending British Muslims amongst others, he had grievously betrayed the generosity of the British government.

Thereafter, Salman Rushdie became fair game for a number of commentators, and stories appeared about the cost to the taxpayer of maintaining the author's security, and demands increased that he should not only delay indefinitely the paperback, but also agree to withdraw the hard-back version of *The Satanic Verses*. Meanwhile, Dr Kalim Siddiqui, leader of a small minority of UK Muslims, publicly endorsed the *fatwa*, urged others to pursue it, retracted and then re-assumed his initial position.

On 17 February 1989, President Khamenei of Iran said that if Salman Rushdie were to repent of his actions in writing and publishing *The Satanic Verses*, it was possible that people might pardon him. During the 1,000 days since then, Salman Rushdie has explicitly and publicly apologised for any offence he might have caused Muslims no less than five times. On each occasion, the apology, together with his halting of any production of the English-language paperback edition of *The Satanic Verses*, has been rapidly and unequivocally rejected by the Iranian authorities.

This chronology records the destruction of property by fire and bombings; the riots in many countries over *The Satanic Verses* in which people have died and many have been injured. The toll is tragic, shocking and unacceptable. One must, however, question who perpetrated these killings and for what reasons? Do books cause deaths? They do not. But those who wish to impose religious or political views all too often *use* books to *create* unrest and injury to further their cause.

The International Committee believes, and will continue to argue, that to accede to the demands for the total withdrawal of *The Satanic Verses* will not resolve the issue. It will not make the world a safer place to live in; in fact to do so can only make it more profitable in the long-run for any group, anywhere, to issue death threats when their beliefs or opinions are challenged.

In common with all governments, the UK government not only has the duty to protect one of its citizens under such a threat, but a positive duty to uphold the principle of freedom of expression upon which democracy rests. This means maintaining strong diplomatic pressure on the Iranian government and public refutation of the *fatwa* and the reward for Salman Rushdie's death until the death threat is removed. The words of the US Ambassador testifying to the

Senate Foreign Relations Committee on March 8 1989 still hold: "Any real concession to terrorists begets more terrorism."

Frances D'Souza
Director Article 19
Chairperson ICDSR

One Thousand Days

in a Balloon

Salman Rushdie

A hot-air balloon drifts slowly over a bottomless chasm, carrying several passengers. A leak develops; the balloon starts
losing height. The pit, a dark yawn, comes closer. Good
grief! The wounded balloon can bear just one passenger to
safety; the many must be sacrificed to save the one! But who
should live, who should die? And who could make such a
choice?

In point of fact, debating societies everywhere regularly
make such choices without qualms, for of course what I've
described is the given situation of that evergreen favourite,
the Balloon Debate, in which, as the speakers argue over the
relative merits and demerits of the well-known figures they
have placed in disaster's mouth, the assembled company
blithely accepts the faintly unpleasant idea that a human
being's right to life is increased or diminished by his or her
virtues or vices – that we may be born equal but thereafter
our lives weigh differently in the scales.

It's only make-believe, after all. And while it may not be
very nice, it does reflect how people actually think.

I have now spent over a thousand days in just such a balloon; but, alas, this isn't a game. For most of these thousand
days, my fellow-travellers included the Western hostages in
the Lebanon, and the British businessmen imprisoned in
Iran and Iraq, Roger Cooper and Ian Richter. And I had to
accept, and did accept, that for most of my countrymen and
countrywomen, my plight counted for less than the others'.
In any choice between us, I'd have been the first to be
pitched out of the basket and into the abyss. "Our lives
teach us who we are," I wrote at the end of my essay "In
Good Faith". Some of the lessons have been harsh, and difficult to learn.

Trapped inside a metaphor, I've often felt the need to
redescribe it, to change the terms. This isn't so much a balloon, I've wanted to say, as a bubble, within which I'm

simultaneously exposed and sealed off. The bubble floats above and through the world, depriving me of reality, reducing me to an abstraction. For many people, I've ceased to be a human being. I've become an issue, a bother, an "affair". Bullet-proof bubbles, like this one, are reality-proof, too. Those who travel in them, like those who wear Tolkien's rings of invisibility, become wraith-like if they're not careful. They get lost. In this phantom space a man may become the bubble that encases him, and then one day – pop! – he's gone forever.

It's ridiculous – isn't it? – to have to say, "But I *am* a human being, unjustly accused, unjustly embubbled." Or is it I who am being ridiculous, as I call out from my bubble, *"I'm still trapped in here, folks; somebody, please, get me out?"*

Out there where you are, in the rich and powerful and lucky West, has it really been so long since religions persecuted people, burning them as heretics, drowning them as witches, that you can't recognize religious persecution when you see it?... The original metaphor has reasserted itself. I'm back in the balloon, asking for the right to live.

What is my single life worth? Despair whispers in my ear: "Not a lot." But I refuse to give in to despair.

I refuse to give in to despair because I've been shown love as well as hatred. I know that many people do care, and are appalled by the crazy, upside-down logic of the post-*fatwa* world, in which a single novelist can be accused of having savaged or "mugged" a whole community, becoming its tormentor (instead of its tarred and feathered victim) and the scapegoat for all its discontents. Many people do ask, for example: When a white pop-star-turned-Islamic-fanatic speaks approvingly about killing an Indian immigrant, how does the Indian immigrant end up being called the racist?

Or, again: What minority is smaller and weaker than a minority of one?

I refuse to give in to despair even though, for a thousand days and more, I've been put through a degree course in worthlessness, my own personal and specific worthlessness. My first teachers were the mobs marching down distant boulevards, baying for my blood, and finding, soon enough, their echoes on English streets. I could not understand the force that makes parents hang murderous slogans around their children's necks. I have learned to understand it. It burns books and effigies and thinks itself holy. But at first, as I watched the marchers, I felt them trampling on my heart.

Once again, however, I have been saved by instances of fair-mindedness, of goodness. Every time I learn that a reader somewhere has been touched by *The Satanic Verses*, moved and entertained and stimulated by it, it arouses deep feelings in me. And there are more and more such readers nowadays, my post-bag tells me, readers (including Muslims) who are willing to give my burned, spurned child a fair hearing at long last. Milan Kundera writes to say that he finds great tenderness towards Muslim culture in the book, and I'm stupidly grateful. A Muslim writes to say that in spite of the book's "shock tactics" its ideas about the birth of Islam are very positive; at once, I find myself wishing upon a star that her co-religionists may somehow, impossibly, come to agree with her.

Sometimes I think that, one day, Muslims will be ashamed of what Muslims did in these times, will find the "Rushdie affair" as improbable as the West now finds martyr-burning. One day they may agree that – as the European Enlightenment demonstrated – freedom of thought is precisely freedom from religious control, freedom from accusations of blasphemy. Maybe they'll agree, too, that the row over *The Satanic Verses* was at bottom an argument about who should have the power of the grand narrative, the Story of Islam, and that that power must belong equally to everyone. That even if my novel were incompetent, its attempt to retell the Story would still be important. That if I've failed, others must succeed, because those who do not have power over the story that dominates their lives, power to retell it, rethink it, deconstruct it, joke about it, and change it as times change, truly are powerless, because they cannot think new thoughts.

One day. Maybe. But not today.

Today, my education in worthlessness continues, and

what Saul Bellow would call my "reality instructors" include: the media pundit who suggests that a manly death would be better for me than hiding like a rat; the letter-writer who points out that of course the trouble is that I *look* like the Devil, and wonders if I have hairy shanks and cloven hooves; the "moderate" Muslim who writes to say that Muslims find it "revolting" when I speak about the Iranian death threats (it's not the *fatwa* that's revolting, you understand, but my mention of it); the rather more immoderate Muslim who tells me to "shut up", explaining that if a fly is caught in a spider's web, it should not attract the attention of the spider. I ask the reader to imagine how it might feel to be intellectually and emotionally bludgeoned, from a thousand different directions, every day for a thousand days and more.

Back in the balloon, something longed-for and heartening has happened. On this occasion, *mirabile dictu*, the many have not been sacrificed, but saved. That is to say, my companions, the Western hostages and the jailed businessmen, have by good fortune and the efforts of others managed to descend safely to earth, and have been reunited with their families and friends, with their own, free lives. I rejoice for them, and admire their courage, their resilience. And now I'm alone in the balloon.

Surely I'll be safe now? Surely, now, the balloon will drop safely towards some nearby haven, and I, too, will be reunited with my life? Surely it's my turn now?

But the balloon is over the chasm again; and it's still sinking. I realize that it's carrying a great deal of valuable freight. Trading relations, armaments deals, the balance of power in the Gulf – these and other matters of great moment are weighing down the balloon. I hear voices suggesting that if I stay aboard, the precious cargo will be endangered. The national interest is being redefined; am I being redefined out of it? Am I to be jettisoned, after all?

When Britain renewed relations with Iran at the United Nations in 1990, the senior British official in charge of the negotiations assured me in unambiguous language that something very substantial had been achieved on my behalf. The Iranians, laughing merrily, had secretly agreed to forget the *fatwa*. (The diplomat telling me the story put great stress on this cheery Iranian laughter.) They would "neither encourage nor allow" their citizens, surrogates, or proxies to act against me. Oh, how I wanted to believe that! But in the year-and-a-bit that followed, we saw the *fatwa* restated in Iran, the bounty money doubled, the book's Italian translator severely wounded, its Japanese translator stabbed to death; there was news of an attempt to find and kill me by contract killers working directly for the Iranian government through its European embassies. Another such contract was successfully carried out in Paris, the victim being the harmless and aged ex-Prime Minister of Iran, Shapour Bakhtiar.

It seems reasonable to deduce that the secret deal made at the United Nations hasn't worked. Dismayingly, however, the talk as I write is all of improving relations with Iran still further, while the "Rushdie case" is described as a side-issue.

Is this a balloon I'm in, or the dustbin of history?

Let me be clear: *there is nothing I can do to break this impasse*. The *fatwa* was politically motivated to begin with, it remains a breach of international law, and it can only be solved at the political level. To effect the release of the Western hostages in the Lebanon, great levers were moved, great forces were brought into play; for Mr Richter, seventy million pounds in frozen Iraqi assets were "thawed". What, then, is a novelist under terrorist attack worth?

Despair murmurs, once again: "Not a plugged nickel."

But I refuse to give in to despair.

You may ask why I'm so sure there's nothing I can do to help myself out of this jam.

At the end of 1990, dispirited and demoralized, feeling abandoned, even then, in consequence of the British government's decision to patch things up with Iran, and with my marriage at an end, I faced my deepest grief, my unquenchable sorrow at having been torn away from, cast out of, the cultures and societies from which I'd always drawn my strength and inspiration – that is, the broad community of British Asians, and the broader community of

19

Indian Muslims. I determined to make my peace with Islam, even at the cost of my pride. Those who were surprised and displeased by what I did perhaps failed to see that I was not some deracinated Uncle Tom Wog. To these people it was apparently incomprehensible that I should seek to make peace between the warring halves of the world, which were also the warring halves of my soul – and that I should seek to do so in a spirit of humility, instead of the arrogance so often attributed to me.

In "In Good Faith" I wrote: "Perhaps a way forward might be found through the mutual recognition of [our] mutual pain," but even moderate Muslims had trouble with this notion: what pain, they asked, could I possibly have suffered? *What was I talking about?* As a result, the really important conversations I had in this period were with myself.

I said: Salman, you must send a message loud enough to be heard all over the world. You must make ordinary Muslims see that you aren't their enemy, and make the West understand a little more of the complexity of Muslim cultures. It was my hope that Westerners might say, well, if he's the one in danger, and yet he's willing to acknowledge the importance of his Muslim roots, then perhaps we ought to start thinking a little less stereotypically ourselves. (No such luck, though. The message you send isn't always the one that's received.)

And I said to myself: Admit it, Salman, the Story of Islam has a deeper meaning for you than any of the other grand narratives. Of course you're no mystic, mister, and when you wrote *I am not a Muslim* that's what you meant. No supernaturalism, no literalist orthodoxies, no formal rules for you. But Islam doesn't have to mean blind faith. It can mean what it always meant in your family: a culture, a civilization, as open-minded as your grandfather was, as delightedly disputatious as your father was, as intellectual and philosophical as you like. Don't let the zealots make *Muslim* a terrifying word, I urged myself; remember when it meant *family* and *light*.

I reminded myself that I had always argued that it was necessary to develop the nascent concept of the "secular

Muslim", who, like the secular Jews, affirmed his member-
ship of the culture while being separate from the theology. I
had recently read the contemporary Muslim philosopher
Fouad Zakariya's *Laïcité ou Islamisme*, and been encouraged
by Zakariya's attempt to modernize Islamic thought. But,
Salman, I told myself, you can't argue from outside the
debating chamber. You've got to cross the threshold, go
inside the room, and *then* fight for your humanized, historicized, secularized way of being a Muslim. I recalled my near-
namesake, the twelfth-century philosopher Ibn Rushd
(Averroës), who argued that (to quote the great Arab historian Albert Hourani), "not all the words of the Qur'an
should be taken literally. When the literal meaning of
Qur'anic verses appeared to contradict the truths to which
philosophers arrived by the exercise of reason, those verses
needed to be interpreted metaphorically." But Ibn Rushd
was a snob. Having propounded an idea far in advance of
its time, he qualified it by saying that such sophistication
was only suitable for the élite; literalism would do for the
masses. Salman, I asked myself, is it time to pick up Ibn
Rushd's banner and carry it forward; to say, nowadays such
ideas are fit for everybody, for the beggar as well as the
prince?

It was with such things in mind – and with my thoughts in
a state of some confusion and torment – that I spoke the
Muslim creed before witnesses. But my fantasy of joining
the fight for the modernization of Muslim thought, for freedom from the shackles of the Thought Police, was stillborn.
It never really had a chance. Too many people had spent
too long demonizing or totemizing me to listen seriously to
what I had to say. In the West, some "friends" turned
against me, calling me by yet another set of insulting names.
Now I was spineless, pathetic, debased; I had betrayed
myself, my Cause; above all, I had betrayed *them*.

I also found myself up against the granite, heartless cer-
tainties of Actually Existing Islam, by which I mean the
political and priestly power structure that presently dominates and stifles Muslim societies. Actually Existing Islam
has failed to create a free society anywhere on Earth, and it

wasn't about to let me, of all people, argue in favour of one. Suddenly I was (metaphorically) among people whose social attitudes I'd fought all my life – for example, their attitudes about women (one Islamicist boasted to me that his wife would cut his toe-nails while he made telephone calls, and suggested I found such a spouse), or about gays (one of the Imams I met in December 1990 was on TV soon afterwards, denouncing Muslim gays as sick creatures who brought shame on their families and who ought to seek medical and psychiatric help). Had I truly fallen in among such people? *That was not what I meant at all.*

Facing the utter intransigence, the Philistine scorn of so much of Actually Existing Islam, I reluctantly concluded that there was no way for me to help bring into being the Muslim culture I'd dreamed of, the progressive, irreverent, sceptical, argumentative, playful and *unafraid* culture which is what I've always understood as *freedom*. Not me, not in this lifetime, no chance. Actually Existing Islam, which has all but deified its Prophet, a man who always fought passionately against such deification; which has supplanted a priest-free religion by a priest-ridden one; which makes literalism a weapon and redescriptions a crime, will never let the likes of me in.

Ibn Rushd's ideas were silenced in their time. And throughout the Muslim world today, progressive ideas are in retreat. Actually Existing Islam reigns supreme, and just as the recently destroyed "Actually Existing Socialism" of the Soviet terror-state was horrifically unlike the utopia of peace and equality of which democratic socialists have dreamed, so also is Actually Existing Islam a force to which I have never given in, to which I cannot submit.

There is a point beyond which conciliation looks like capitulation. I do not believe I passed that point, but others have thought otherwise.

I have never disowned my book, nor regretted writing it. I said I was sorry to have offended people, because I had not set out to do so, and so I am. I explained that writers do not agree with every word spoken by every character they create – a truism in the world of books, but a continuing mystery to *The Satanic Verses'* opponents. I have always said that this novel has been traduced. Indeed, the chief benefit of my meeting with six Islamic scholars on Christmas Eve 1990 was that they agreed that the novel had no insulting motives. "In Islam, it is a man's intention that counts," I was told. "Now we will launch a worldwide campaign on your behalf to explain that there has been a great mistake." All this with much smiling and friendliness and handshaking. It was in this context that I agreed to suspend – not cancel – a paperback edition, to create what I called a space for reconciliation.

Alas, I overestimated these men. Within days all but one of them had broken their promises, and recommenced to vilify me and my work as if we had not shaken hands. I felt (most probably I had been) a great fool. The suspension of the paperback began at once to look like a surrender. In the aftermath of the attacks on my translators, it looks even more craven. It has now been more than three years since *The Satanic Verses* was published; that's a long, long "space for reconciliation". Long enough. I accept that I was wrong to have given way on this point. *The Satanic Verses* must be freely available and easily affordable, if only because if it is not read and studied, then these years will have no meaning. Those who forget the past are condemned to repeat it.

"Our lives teach us who we are." I have learned the hard way that when you permit anyone else's description of reality to supplant your own – and such descriptions have been raining down on me, from security advisers, governments, journalists, archbishops, friends, enemies, mullahs – then you might as well be dead. Obviously, a rigid, blinkered, absolutist world-view is the easiest to keep hold of; whereas the fluid, uncertain, metamorphic picture I've always carried about is rather more vulnerable. Yet I must cling with all my might to that chameleon, that chimera, that shape-shifter, my own soul; must hold on to its mischievous, icon-oclastic, out-of-step clown-instincts, no matter how great the storm. And if that plunges me into contradiction and para-dox, so be it; I've lived in that messy ocean all my life. I've fished in it for my art. This turbulent sea was the sea outside my bedroom window in Bombay. It is the sea by which I was born, and which I carry within me wherever I go.

"Free speech is a non-starter," says one of my Islamic extremist opponents. No, sir, it is not. Free speech is the whole thing, the whole ball game. Free speech is life itself.

That's the end of my speech from this ailing balloon. Now it's time to answer the question. What is my single life worth?

Is it worth more or less than the fat contracts and political treaties that are in here with me? Is it worth more or less than good relations with a country which, in April 1991, gave 800 women seventy-four lashes each for not wearing a veil; in which the eighty-year-old writer Mariam Firouz is still in jail, and has been tortured; and whose Foreign Minister says, in response to criticism of his country's lamentable human rights record, "International monitoring of the human rights situation in Iran should not continue indefinitely ... Iran could not tolerate such monitoring for long"?

You must decide what you think a friend is worth to his friends, what you think a son is worth to his mother, or a father to his son. You must decide what a man's conscience and heart and soul are worth. You must decide what you think a writer is worth, what value you place on a maker of stories and an arguer with the world.

Ladies and gentlemen, the balloon is sinking into the abyss.

Letters to
Salman Rushdie

Günter Grass

Dear Salman Rushdie,

In your essay "One Thousand Days in a Balloon" one cannot miss the plea for support and, at the end, the desperately loud cry for help – "the balloon is sinking into the abyss". Nevertheless, I fear that the multitude of threatening events crowding in hardly allows for an overview any more, let alone insight. It will drown out your cry – especially in Germany, where the unity of the nation that has been claimed during the past year is beginning to be affected with painful self-obsession. "Do not disturb." Moreover, great migrations of people who want to nibble at our wealth are threatening from the east and the south. We, as descendants of Germanic tribesmen, know how good we were on our feet in olden times. And that's why we know what it is we need to warn against, and what it is we need to recommend: fortress Europe!

What do the self-righteous care about the plea of a writer, who as an Indian claims to be British and on top of that has himself to blame for his admittedly fatal situation. This murder threat made almost three years ago. Unpleasant, barbaric and worthy of condemnation. But what more could one do? And spoken among hypocrites: could this man Rushdie not have written more quietly, more accommodatingly and, given all his talent, with more consideration? And then the far too provocative title of the book, *The SATANIC Verses*!

I'm not exaggerating. I've experienced this willed and selective deafness, half-agonized, half-embarrased, often enough, most recently on the occasion of the Frankfurt Book Fair, when the German economics minister was working to foster – in Tehran of all places – a favourable climate for his large-scale projects, and the management of the Frankfurt Book Fair wanted, obligingly, to support him.

And yet, dear Salman, you are not alone. This letter and, as I hope, further letters are an attempt to give your place of exile, the metaphorical gondola, a lift. More than that: I would like, if you permit me, to be your guest, your fellow traveller, for a while. Even if we should not be able to evoke once again the easy affinity and good humour of our first meeting – it was at the time of the publication of the German edition of *Midnight's Children* – a closeness as writers has remained and with it a pleasure in the sense and nonsense of acrobatic word play. Perhaps the picture which illustrated your plea "One Thousand Days in a Balloon" in *Die Zeit*, Max Beckmann's *High Wire Artists*, can help us out. In this painting a smiling lady waving a little flag looks out of the gondola, from which a man seems to be falling head first. And yet, in the manner of acrobats, he is still holding on by his feet, so that he will be ready to blow into Beckmann's favourite instrument, the trumpet, which he is carrying with him: a march or chorale, the blues or trumpet-calls, in any case blasts which will put wind behind the balloon.

Are not such pictures what give us courage in a desperate situation? Pictures which do not avoid horror, which do not gloss over anything, whose poetry bears every ordeal?

At the end of the year I saw on television, among the usual and by now daily announcements of catastrophes, a report from the frontline of the Serbo-Croatian civil war. Since it was the time of the most Christian festival in the calendar, a Croat soldier was decorating a Christmas tree by hanging hand grenades on the branches: ridged, decorative fruits waiting to be cracked open. Who dares cry blasphemy, sacrilege? I don't know what thoughts moved this soldier. I assume that as long as the camera was pointing, he carried on his activity with particular concentration. If the camera man was not satisfied, perhaps he had to repeat his decorative work several times. And yet intentionally as well as unintentionally, he succeeded in giving expression to the very latest barbarity of his time, of our time. He could not have decorated the Christmas tree more truthfully. I am certain: the man from Nazareth, about thirty years old and still youthful, this gentle rebel and angry purifier of the Temple, well-versed in scripture and opposed to all high-priestly dogmatists, this man who has come down to us as Jesus Christ and who, as revolutionary troublemaker has for safety's sake been imprisoned in churches, would have had no objections to the hand grenades on the Christmas tree. Jesus Christ loved to provoke. Which is why I am also sure that the man called Muhammad, who has come down to us as Prophet, would have read the novels of the writer Salman Rushdie, and especially *The Satanic Verses*, with pleasure.

Beckmann's trumpeter, seeming to fall out of the gondola, and the soldier decorating the Christmas tree with hand grenades are our brothers. Who else, Salman, who else? We know about priests and politicians. They are not to be trusted. Their actions are far from disinterested. When the Gulf War began a year ago, both sides thought they knew exactly what good is and what evil is. So they both acted, respectively, in God's name. The result was murderous, and the dead were left uncounted.

In your plea, "One Thousand Days in a Balloon", you talk about "security advisers, governments, journalists, archbishops, friends, enemies, mullahs", who hold on tight to the "rigid, blinkered, absolutist world-view" and want to impose it on you. Against it you set the "fluid, uncertain, the metamorphic picture", which you have carried within you all your life, which makes you vulnerable. In the end you insist that you must continue to stand by the "shape-shifter" of your own soul and by its "mischievous, iconoclastic, out-of-step clown-instincts". You talk about a "messy ocean" in which you have fished for your art and once again evoke the turbulent sea below the city of Bombay. "It is the sea by which I was born, and which I carry within me wherever I go."

Many years ago, dear Salman, we conducted a conversation for television about your lost Bombay and my lost Danzig, among other things. We recognized that through our common experience loss has made us eloquent. Loss is the condition of our stories. So let us continue fishing for words, you in the dirty, turbulent Indian Ocean, I in my poisoned Baltic, for words that stand in the way and tell of many realities, that will not tolerate as the only valid reality the one which is forced on us.

I hope you know that I am trying to live your daily anxieties and illusory hopes with you, also your courage won from fear.

I send my greatings to you up in the balloon.

Günter Grass

Paul Theroux

Dear Salman,

I swear I thought it was a joke – a very bad joke, a bit like Papa Doc Duvalier putting a voodoo curse on Graham Greene for writing *The Comedians*, but a joke nevertheless, in the sense of being no more than an example of furious but harmless flatulence – just wind.

Now I can hardly believe that three years have passed since we sat at that memorial service in London for Bruce Chatwin, the day your death sentence was handed down by the Ayatollah Khomeini – Valentine's Day, 1989. The so-called *fatwa*, which had no precedent, and no legal basis, nothing behind it except the fanatic bluster of a clergyman of low repute, seemed at the time so ludicrous to me, so utterly absurd, so remote from anything rational or humane that, as the priests chanted in Greek and swung their thuribums and incense pots, I whispered to you, "You're next, Salman!"

I thought your death sentence would be laughed off – I expected it to be condemned as despicable, and then mocked. Of course, I did not foresee much merriment about *The Satanic Verses* in any Islamic state, where building blueprints have to be submitted to the *ulema* so that the authorities can make sure that no toilet faces Mecca. Where toys and calendars and mugs based on the Muppet figure of "Miss Piggy" are dragged from shops by the religious police (the *mutawaiin*) and ritually destroyed. Where (in Saudi Arabia) women are banned from driving cars because (and this is the official justification) woman cannot be trusted to go anywhere alone. Where they can't read Orwell's *Animal Farm* because the central characters are fairly intelligent pigs. Where if you break wind during prayers, the Islamic rule is that you have to start praying all over again – the fart sort of taints the entire prayer. Where there are equally batty and murderous-sounding *fatwas*, such as the recent one delivered by a Saudi official cleric, Sheikh Abdallah bin Abdelrahman al-Jabrin, which declared that as all Shiite Muslims are heretics they should all be killed. Where beheadings for adultery and hands chopped off for theft are common occurrences.

You know you have travelled through the looking-glass when you are in a country where Miss Piggy is seen as the very embodiment of evil. But we were in London, Salman!

When we left the church your face was blank with apprehension, you were cornered by some journalists, hurried away, and I haven't seen you since.

After that, there was all sorts of equivocation – even British politicians saying your book should have been banned. They helped sink you. And W.H. Smith Ltd., the chain of British newsagents that makes a fortune selling pornographic magazines, refused to stock your novel. Shops that did stock it did not advertise it, and although you sold many copies, has anyone ever seen a person reading it in a public place?

How disgusting to see that so far the intimidation of fanatics has worked: you are in hiding, your book is still vilified, your life is still threatened. Most countries, including your own – Britain – are doing business with Iran, buying their oil and their carpets and their cashew nuts, and selling them video machines and new cars and wrist-watches, sending them paper and ink so they can print their fatuous laws. Trading partners in Europe and America are treating the Islamic Republic of Iran as though it is a civilized and rational place, when any fool can see that the Ayatollah's *fatwa* is barbarous and ignorant, as well as, from the point of view of international law, an example of criminal incitement.

While you have been holed up I have been travelling – and I have been well aware of my freedom and your confinement. I have been island-hopping in the Pacific for the past two and a half years, free as a bird, but you have been on my mind. About a year ago I was in Fiji – off the beaten path, on the big jungly island of Vanua Levu. I ran into a Muslim in a rotting coastal village and after we talked a bit I asked him whether he had heard of you. He said, "Yes.

Rushdie is a bad man."

In Sydney, Australia, one my taxi drivers was an economic refugee from Pakistan, a man of sixty, with a science degree from Karachi U. We talked about the Koran for a while, and then I popped the question. His bony hands tightened on the steering wheel: "Rushdie must die."

Naturally I set these people straight. I suggested to them that these were ignorant and barbarous sentiments. And I mentioned them to your Australian publishers. These big strong Australians, living in a democratic country, with a tradition of rugged individualism and talent for being rude, said confidentially that they were frightened. One said, "Some of us have families."

This is all very discouraging. On a personal level people are muddled or uninterested; on an official and governmental level, the response has been weak and cowardly; on a religious level, the Muslims have either been supine or vindictive.

Enough of this. There is very little that you can do, Salman. The task is for the rest of us who have to resist the notion that beheadings and ritual toy destruction and the correct orientation of toilets are rational and humane, or that the religious leader in one country has the power to condemn the citizen of another country to death, for writing a book. Yet it always struck me as distinctly odd when British and American academics willingly went to any number of Islamic countries and taught in schools where women are segregated from men, and the laws are medieval (in Damascus these days, Jews are forbidden to travel more than 2km from their houses in the ghetto). They did it for the money.

And the governments which have been timid in defending your rights have been influenced by money considerations, too. They need to see you as you are, a hostage to much worse fanaticism than confined Terry Anderson or John McCarthy. It is not just the Hezbollah but the entire Muslim world that has been urged to kill you.

The first step is for governments and world leaders to speak out on your behalf.

Then it is our turn – the readers and writers. It is obvious that if any of us raises your name in Iran or Saudi Arabia or Pakistan – or like-minded countries – you will be vilified and we will be hounded. But this ought not to be the case in the rest of the world. Any non-Muslim country with the rule of law ought to be a safe haven for you, where you can walk the streets and ride the buses and live your life without fear of being set upon.

Muslims who might take it into their heads to try and harm you need to be reminded of this. Therefore, it is for them, especially the leaders of Muslim communities in Europe and America, to speak out in your defence and to condemn the *fatwa* as criminal incitement. Muslims living in democratic countries have a duty to condemn the *fatwa* – or else why linger in a land of unbelievers? Speaking as an American, I would be very worried if the Bill of Rights were in danger of being replaced by the *Shari'a*.

It is awkward to be talking about Muslims this way, because Islam is one of the world's great religions, and many of its tenets are humane. But Muslims who do not understand that the *fatwa* is an aberration must be singled out, because only they pose a threat to you.

With your confinement in mind, I have made a point of asking every Muslim I meet – no matter who – their views on you and your book. I have had some crisp replies, but still think my little practice is salutary. In the recent past, white South Africans were always asked about Mandela, and about apartheid in general. And these days, Israelis are – as they ought to be – asked their views on the Palestinian question.

It ought to happen everywhere: first the question – *What about Rushdie?* – and if the answer is hostile, set them straight. This should also happen on an official level, whenever a world leader communicates with President Rafsanjani. *What about Rushdie?* I have no doubt that eventually the message will get through, and you will be free.

Take care, my friend.

Paul Theroux

Arnold Wesker

My Dear Salman,

We have been asked to write a letter to you. I'll wager that most of us are speechless. My house is yours, my time is yours, my outrage is yours, but what is there left to say concerning your Escher nightmare in which the geometry of argument and consolation doesn't make sense? We lose our way, walk up steps which stand us on our heads, end where we began.

I would sooner meet with you and talk about the kind of subjects we did when we last met. Do you remember? You claimed that imaginations were at work in the world of science matched by few in the world of literature. I'm not sure I agree. I share your wide eyes over science but in a way there's something too easy in our excitement because the nature of science renders *every* new discovery an amazing thrill. What was it like to ride the first wheel or look at the stars through the first magnifying glass? Jane Austen, the Brontës, George Elliot weren't really overshadowed by electricity or the internal combustion engine. Stunning though Hawking's quest may be for the one equation to explain all, it is not going to turn me away in disappointment from either Philip Roth's *Counterlife* or your *Satanic Verses*. Nevertheless I was grateful in that conversation to have been informed by you about Gleick's book of the new science of "Chaos". Its contents became a drive in one of my latest plays.

This is what it seems to me I must write to you about: things normal, as though all was right in your world. My response to your adversaries whose madness deems your sanity criminal is to insist upon your normality. All other responses are known! The arguments about the right to dissent have been laid out, the furies have been expressed, the threats made, the unbridgeable divides identified. What

35

remains is to treat you as though you were making your normal way in the world. To come and go and be embraced in our homes is the only response we can make to those warriors of a God they misunderstand.

It's not satisfactory, though, is it? Too much that is urgent is being left unsaid. And so, Escher-like, we return to where we began: what exactly *is* being left unsaid? That those warriors on the irreligious fringes of rebellion have us – especially you poor-innocent-believing-all-humankind-was-reasonable – by the balls? It's known. That the *fatwa* offends us deeply in some corner of our being that is terrified by dormant childhood fears named Certitude, Bigotry, and Irrationality? It's known. That you are in anguish and need our moral support? It's known. Anger and commiseration are futile.

That's our problem – there's no room or point for further debate. All is known. Humankind has since Adam thrown up its fervourists who not only claim possession of the truth but feel threatened to the point of murder if their truths are countered. There is no assuaging them because it's not their faith which is questioned but their *raison d'être*. To disagree with them is tantamount, they imagine, to wishing them dead. Who can debate with such people? Which is why we feel speechless. And helpless. And futile.

In that play which I just mentioned to you, where chaos features, a shadow-cabinet minister is being interviewed on TV. Here is his answer to one of the questions put to him by the interviewer:

There is no doubt in my mind that the three major issues to confront the 21st century will be world poverty, environment, and a conflict between believers and non-believers...

... take the problem of the conflict between religious fanaticism and religious tolerance. Voltaire thought it was solved 250 years ago when the age of reason dawned over Europe, but reason and tolerance didn't, like spring, burst out all over. Now, why? We have to be able to identify the spiritual bacteria that inflame bigotry. Or do we just pacify religious states with a kind of soothing, there-there-we-love-you diplomacy? Is education the answer to fanaticism? Or must we make damn sure we've got a military

defence against holy wars? Here's a formulation which I think should be printed as huge posters and stuck on walls all over the world:

My respect for your liberty to live and pray and believe as you wish does not mean I have to respect what *you believe,* how you *live or the* content *of your prayers.*

Stay warm, calm, creative, and confident in the knowledge that most of the best and kindest minds are behind you – though you might wish to God they were in front! I know you didn't ask to be the fulcrum of one of the severest conflicts pulling our times apart, but there it is – you have made history which in turn is making you. Islam is here forever. My hope is that your work has given courage to Islam's wisest to stand up against its powerful simpletons.

I send my love and respect to you whom I consider a hero of our time.

Arnold Wesker

Margaret Atwood

Dear Salman Rushdie,

Right now I'm staying in Southern France. Only a few kilometres away from here there's a spur of rock that was a fort for several millennia. At the tip of it there's a carved basin, used by the Celto-Ligurians for chopping off sacrificial heads.

It's a very old belief, this notion that God is an angry vampire who requires human blood – old, entrenched and hard to get rid of, as the history of the Middle Ages here amply demonstrates. This area was the scene of much heterodoxy, and also of much bloodshed. The Cathars made their last stand here; the Vaudois, somewhat later, were tortured, raped, mutilated and slaughtered here in large numbers; and the Hugenots were strong in this region until after after the revocation of the Edict of Nantes, when France became so dangerous for them that it was known as "The Desert". And every butchery, every torture, was sanctimoniously perpetrated in the name of God, which casts a certain lurid light on the sweet Christmas crèches in the local stores and the grateful *ex votos* in the local churches. But then, is any religion invalidated by its extremists, and by those who use it cynically to consolidate their own power? If so, most of them – and most of us – are in deep trouble.

Which is a prelude. The other day I was thinking back to the time when I first read your book. It had just been published, and I was reading eagerly along, when I came across the section which has since caused all the uproar. At that moment a very small wisp of doubt drifted across my brain. "Could it be," I thought, "that this is going to seriously disturb some Muslims?" But no, I thought: this passage is meant to be part of a dream, taking place in the head of a character who is a reprobate. No reader could possibly confuse it with the real opinions of the author of the book.

Well, I've been wrong before but this time I was spectacularly wrong. Coming as I do from a soul-searching Protestant background, I gave some thought – after the demonstrations, after the *fatwa*, after the events that have made you so indelibly and lamentably historic – to the reason for my own wrongness. Some of it was due, no doubt, to the kind of fatuous optimism that leads me to believe that everyone reads books with care and thoroughness and an attention to irony and subtlety – though, as every writer knows, many a critic can't even get the plot straight, much less the point – but part of it surely came from my rootedness, as a reader, in the heterogeneity of Christian tradition.

Christianity as a house has many mansions, which is linked to the fact that its sacred text, the Bible, did not appear at one time and in one place, and was not even written in one language; instead it accumulated. Its shape comes from an arrangement of disparate parts – family trees, poetry, songs, drama, narratives of many kinds – rather than from a unity of one will, one style, one impulse. The way of reading it that evolved over the centuries was similarly polyphonal: to make sense of the book, it had to be. Every sacred element had its counterparts in the secular and demonic worlds, every Type has its Anti-type. For Christ there was the Anti-Christ, for the Tree of Life there was the Tree of Death, for the Garden there was the Desert, for the Virgin Mary there was the Scarlet Woman. Anti-types or demonic parodies might take the same outward form as the sacred Types, but their content – their spiritual polarity – was upside down.

As a culture, Christianity has shown a tendency to allow this upside-downess; by *allow*, I mean that it has allowed it to have its say, it was given a voice and a role. It was in fact part of the divine drama: without the Devil there would have been no Fall, and no Redemption. The Devil's Advocate was a necessary personage in mediaeval Church trials, demonic gargoyles with horns and bat-wings leer down from cathedral roofs, and there are imps and satirical grotesques within the churches themselves. And in the calendar of the Church, odd festivals find place, most notably that of Mardi Gras, when the normal order of things is turned on its head and the dignified and powerful are mocked.

So – since literary criticism, in the West, is the child of Biblical exegesis – that is how I read and understood your book. The Prophet figure was not diminished for having been shown to be human, that is, temptable, since Christ himself was tempted; and the women who took the names of the Prophet's wives were, for me, Anti-types. A wrong reading? Quite possibly; but less wrong, I hope, than one that would mistake every word as a supposed proclamation of literal truth.

These were some of my explanations for my own earlier purblindness – explanations that became increasingly irrelevant, because it was evident as time went on that your book was not just a victim of a culturally-determined misreading, but had been converted into a highly useful propaganda tool for reasons that had little to do with the book *qua* book. Literary niceties had simply been pulverized. It became even clearer to me why I believe that the union of religion and state – any religion, any state – is potentially the most oppressive combination possible. When a disagreement with temporal power is interpreted as a disagreement with God, then all questioning becomes heresy, and all dissenters are demonized.

It took the Christian West almost two thousand years to come to uneasy terms with its own multiplicity. Those killed on the bone-strewn road towards religious toleration number in the millions, and the after-fires are still flickering. I would like to say that all those deaths counted, in the end, for something. I would like to say that the idea of freedom of conscience, and therefore of speech, won the day. It did, sort of, some places; although this must be cold comfort to you, as you can't go out to buy a loaf of bread without risking your life.

Possibly we don't value a thing unless we know a high price has been paid for it; and in this instance we tend to have forgotten the price. "Freedom of conscience" sounds kind of soppy, until you remember how many died in the process of achieving it. And are still dying: why is it that, nowadays, when a repressive dictatorship takes over anywhere, writers are in the front lines?

Possibly we should have a Tomb of the Unknown Writer, killed in the wars of the imagination. There have been quite a few of them. I hope there will not be more.

Margaret Atwood

Nadine Gordimer

Dear Salman,

Whenever I write something about you, my great hope is that it will be outdated before it gets into print: that the *fatwa* demanding your death will by then have been lifted for ever. I fervently wish that when this letter reaches you, it will belong to the unspeakable ordeal behind you.

Again and again I ask myself and everyone, how has world concern allowed the murderous edict against you to continue year after year? Why have the democratic governments, and in particular the British government, occupying themselves with violations of human rights all over the world, not acted in condemnation of this gross violation? If the life of a single human being is expendable, why have strenuous efforts and endless negotiations been employed, internationally and successfully, on behalf of individual political hostages? Is religious persecution once more tolerated, on the threshold of the twenty-first century, while political persecution is not? Why has Amnesty International not recognized your form of incarceration, which makes the whole world your prison since there is nowhere on earth you could go where the *fatwa* authorizing your death would not defy the law of the land. Why does the United Nations not see you for what you are: the prey and – everyday, everywhere – potential victim of international terrorism? Is international terrorism acceptable so long as it is invoked by a great and respected religion?

I have just been given a present of the *Oxford Dictionary of New Words*. Flipping through it, I suddenly see that *"fatwa"* has now passed into the English language. Here it is, recognized in common usage along with "fast-food" and "fast track", given the cachet of listing in a prestigious dictionary. This can have only one meaning; the *fatwa* is, indeed, acceptable as a fact of life – your life. The etymology of its passing into English is blandly given: "Actually a borrowing from Arabic (in the form of *fetfa* or *fetwa*... the *fatwa* acquired a new currency in the English-language media in February 1989, when Iran's Ayatollah Khomeini issued a *fatwa* sentencing the British writer Salman Rushdie to death for publishing *The Satanic Verses* (1988), a book which many Muslims considered blasphemous and highly offensive. *Fatwa* is a generic term for any legal decision made by a Mufti or other Islamic religious authority, but, because of the *particular context in which the West became familiar with the word,* it is sometimes erroneously thought to mean 'death sentence'." (My italics)

A deadly familiarity. The horror is taken out of intent to murder; semantics reconcile it with everyday experience. It has become codified as incidental knowledge useful for crossword puzzle enthusiasts.

In fact it *is* relevant to our everyday experience, whoever we are, in a different, glaring way that most people won't face. People don't have to be writers in order to be exposed, in their own lives or the future lives of their children, to the threats of fanatics – religious, racist, sexist. An individual may live privately and meek as a mouse, and still, one day, by the colour of his skin or the nature of his personal relationships, or the national origin of his grandfather, become marked for destruction as a pariah; indifference to the specific danger is fatal to the freedom of the general.

As for writers, we who are at special risk, the *fatwa* can never be distanced as something that happens to somebody else. With the powers of international terrorism at the service of fanaticism, northern and southern hemispheres are one hunting ground. This week of your dreadful anniversary I am attending a conference of African writers from all over the continent, and I have just reminded them that what has happened to you concerns *us* and will continue to do so, in African literature as part of worldwide post-colonial literature, for your novel is an innovative exploration of one of the most intense experiences we share, the individual personality in transition between two cultures brought together in that post-colonial world – whose arena is Europe and the Americas, as well as the actual territories they once invaded.

You neither advocated nor called for the taking of life through any character in your novel; the precedent of the *fatwa*, claiming the right to your life, is a crime against humanity that also casts a shadow over the free development of literature everywhere.

Dear Salman, may you be able to tear up this letter as something you no longer have any need of: the support of fellow writers and friends in the horrible ordeal you've lived through with unimaginable courage. May we begin to write to each other from within the world of the imagination, the lovely struggle with capturing the word, where we attempt to make sense of *life*, for ourselves and those who read our books.

With love,

Nadine Gordimer

Jatinder Verma

Dear Salman Rushdie,

Guardians, it is said, are appointed for every community in Hell, to prevent individuals from clambering out of the fiery abyss. For every community *except* South Asians. This is because the latter are quite adept at pulling each other back down into the fires! This joke, prevalent amongst Asians, has become grim reality in the years since 14 February 1989. I refer of course to our relations with one of our fellows, Salman Rushdie.

Let me say at the outset that I am *not* a Muslim, and thus pre-empt the expected dismissal of my views from certain quarters. I am the same "translated man" that Salman has so eloquently anatomized over the past decade: an Asian, first and foremost, in Britain. Before we became Muslims and Hindus and Sikhs and Bengalis and Punjabis and Gujaratis and Indians and Pakistanis and Bangladeshis and Khalistanis, we were (and remain still to all intents and purposes) "Asians" – or "Pakis", to be more blunt.

Two decades of striving to find a voice – striving for the right to articulate our hopes and fears; of trying to exert our *presence* amidst the all-pervasive absence of self-image in the public life of Britain – have resulted, since February 1989, in our return to effective silence; paradoxically, through our own actions. I say "our", when in truth it was only a handful of those who claimed to represent us who, using the language of hell-fire and damnation, first raised the image of Salman as traitor to the community.

That same Salman who, when he won the Booker Prize for *Midnight's Children* in 1981, was a source of pride for us all. When he won, we all became prize-winners: it was possible to believe that our speech could, after all, be heard in this, our adopted land. Here was a man who was willing to speak as himself – an Asian-Immigrant-Paki – and not as

47

some "coconut", brown in skin and yet white inside. And the prize did not seem to lessen the man, drown him in hubris (as was the fear of some). His blistering attack on racism, delivered on the newly-inaugurated Channel 4, articulated once again our own inchoate thoughts about life in Britain. He historicized our lives – located us as more than just the "immigrant phenomena". Primarily, Salman's actions through the '80s demonstrated that to be heard by the mainstream of British life did not necessitate kow-towing to the Establishment.

Now, shamefully, some amongst us would look to him to kow-tow to a similar Establishment (it is an ironic mark of our settlement in Britain that we now possess our own Establishments, our own orthodoxies – though, bereft of real power, these have recourse only to the parochial power of fear and intimidation).

I have felt it necessary to reclaim the pre-St Valentine's Day Salman today since there seems to have been a somer-saulting of sorts over the past two Christmases. In 1990, Salman seemed to confound many of his supporters, including me, with his highly-publicized "conversion". Unable to fully comprehend this change, we were forced to simply "keep faith" with the man as he wrestled to find a way out of his predicament. Last year, with his speech in New York, the old pugnacious Salman seemed to have returned. Yet both events, it seems to me, evidence a simplicity of motive: to find a way out of silence. To be absent from public consciousness is to allow everyone to forget that we have a hostage in our midst.

As the pride in 1981 was a collective pride, so too now is the shame of us all. It was not the white Establishment that incarcerated Salman, *we Asians* have done so. This Judas act now hangs like a garland of shame not only around the necks of all us Asians, but also around those of our future generations as long as Salman remains in protective custody under the threat of the *fatwa*. So long as we continue to treasure this pitiful garland, we will have effectively silenced our hope-laden visions of what life in Britain must mean in an age when the walls have come tumbling down.

As we stand on the threshold of a momentous year for Britain and Europe, I plead with Mr Liaquat Hussain, Dr Hesham El-Essawy, Dr Kalim Siddiqui, Dr Sabir Akhtar, et al. to desist from their continued opposition to Salman Rushdie. Indeed, join with him (and all the rest of the muted Asian majority – which has remained mute amidst the learned phrasings of a few) in demanding the lifting of the *fatwa*; that Salman may live and work amongst us again without perpetually having to look over his shoulder. He belongs to us – a part of that diversity of thought and attitude which is the abiding inheritance bequeathed by our ancient civilizations. His continued incarceration is no victory for your cause: it serves only to confine us all – Muslims and non-Muslims alike – to the silence of the ghetto; where our primary concerns – of unemployment, of unhindered movement across Europe, of equality of opportunity – will remain marginalized. You may feel you have one of your legs in another sense of home. Most of us have no such choice. *This* is home. Join us. Or leave us free to continue the construction of a vision of home where diversity is not calumny. Where neither you, nor your Tebbit counterparts, may foist a "cricket test" upon us.

St Valentine's Day has a two-fold association: it is a day for exchanging words of love, and it also marks the gangland massacre in Chicago in the 1920s! Join us, Mr Laiquat Hussain, Dr Hesham El-Essawy, Dr Kalim Siddiqui, Dr Shabbir Akhtar, et al, in upholding the one and forgoing the possibility of the latter ever recurring.

Jatinder Verma

Peter Carey

Dear Salman,

Some friends were hosting a dinner downtown on the night you spoke at Columbia University. The caterer arrived late, out-of-breath, apologetic – he had been stuck at his previous job up at Columbia: "Rushdie showed up," he said, "the place was swarming with cops. They wouldn't let me out."

I didn't discover that you were in New York City until I picked up the *New York Times* the next day and read: Rushdie Appears in New York. My first response was to admire your courage, my next to wonder about the mid-Atlantic security and, shopkeeper's son that I am, who paid for it. The British government must protect you in Britain but would they protect you in the air? Who did protect you above the Atlantic? How did you fly? And did you have to pay for all those minders' seats yourself?

But of course: you had *appeared*. This was the word that gave the headline its extraordinary *frisson*. Ghosts appear – comets, angels. If you *appeared* – I saw this for the first time – it meant that you were in some way no longer a person. You had become an apparition, less than an apparition – an idea.

The journalist in the *New York Times* wrote about your speech and how, in delivering it, you slowly changed, from this thing called "Rushdie" to a man in pain, and I saw with a shock that you really had become a sort of abstraction.

But at the heart of this abstraction is you, my friend, all alone – a hairy-faced man with canvas shoes and baggy pants and perfect recall of every rock n' roll song from 1955 until I don't know when, a man who likes to sing and laugh and talk, a man so social, so gregarious, that if I had to imagine the one soul on earth who would be most tortured by an endless house arrest, I would have had to summon up someone exactly like you.

Yet if I had imagined you, I doubt that I would have had the wit, or the insight, to see how you would have acquitted yourself, how the predicament you found yourself in would sometimes surround you with an aura of what I am nervous to call wisdom, how you have, as the torture has continued, grown.

I cannot guess what Khomeini intended. He may have tortured you, but he has not diminished you. Indeed, he has only pushed you beyond yourself, made you at once stronger and softer in such a way that, when you are finally permitted to be still long enough, to live the life of a writer again, to know at the beginning of one day where you will be the next, we will all see it there shining through your work.

But I am not trying to make sense of your torture, or to give purpose to the fear, the loneliness of confronting your own face in God knows how many different mirrors in how many different safe houses, cleaning your teeth with a toothbrush a policeman has purchased for you, sleeping in strange beds with musty sheets, in old houses that make strange noises at night, new apartments with loud clocks, rattling refrigerators, heating that is too high or too low, and the distant voices of neighbours you will not meet.

Remember, Salman, how, in 1985, we all talked of going to live in New York City? I thought about it the day I learned you had *appeared*. I imagined you moving out of Columbia University surrounded by guards. You were already contained, locked inside a car. You were still filled with adrenalin from your speech, the applause, the crowd. Policemen sat beside you, on each side, in front. They were hard, tense, smelling of excitement and sweat. The windows were up, the heaters on. Were you on the floor? Were you sitting up? Finally, surely, it was safe to at least *look* at the city you had once hoped to live in, which you had, now, tonight, moved with your courage. So, you looked.

And then you went (however you went, wherever you went, whoever paid) back into the life of being a hostage, guarded, moved continually, a prisoner of Iran, held in a Britain that sometimes seems to be oblivious to the fact that

it has been invaded by a foreign power.
We miss you. We send our love.

Peter Carey

Fahimeh Farsaie

Dear Mr Rushdie,

I don't find it at all easy to write you a letter of solidarity. Why, I ask myself? Am I scared of provoking the Iranian government? Am I frightened of its merciless wrath? As an Iranian writer in exile with Iranian citizenship, do I fear difficulties?

Certainly not, Mr Rushdie!

Not because I am made of different stuff and not at all because I am exceptionally courageous. The simple reason is that in the eyes of the powerful in Iran I have committed so many "crimes" that the fact of being "involved in the Rushdie affair" would not weigh further on my condemnation. I will just mention my latest "crime": the publication of the German translation of my novel *Poisoned Time*, which official Iranian newspapers described as an "anti-Islamic, anti-Iranian" book. You can surely imagine the consequences of such a judgement, Mr Rushdie. So one "sin" more or less does not make my "file" heavier or lighter, I think. That's not the point.

Perhaps I can't really understand the horrible and cruel situation you are in, I wonder; living in fear and panic all the time, hemmed in, constantly under guard, enduring nightmares of persecution, torture and murder and feeling alone and forsaken?

Oh yes. I can very well imagine this dreadful, terrifying situation. I don't even need to make a special effort, it doesn't require special imagination or a particularly sensitive heart. For the simple reason that I experienced this horrible and unbearable situation myself when I suffered persecution, when I had to live in hiding and in flight. I still experience it sometimes in exile.

That's not the reason why I find it so difficult to write to you, Mr Rushdie!

Perhaps, I came to think at last, it has to do with the manner in which you and your colleagues made your appeal. "Please make it clear that we don't accept that a man should be murdered just because he has written a book," you said in the Dorchester Hotel at the prizegiving for your children's book *Haroun and the Sea of Stories* last year, "Almost beseeching, with tears in his eyes," as the news magazine *Spiegel* wrote. You made your request explicitly as if nobody had been murdered for his literary activities before 14 February 1989, the day of Khomeini's death sentence against you. Yes! That's what bothered me when I thought about writing you a letter of solidarity. For I had to remember that a few months after this date many "people", i.e. authors and journalists, were executed and buried in mass graves together with other political prisoners because they had written a book or an article and expressed their own views. To mention just a few names: Amir Nikaiin, Monouchehr Behzadi, Djavid Misani, Abutorab Bagherzadeh... They followed the bitter fate of their young colleagues who had been kidnapped, tortured and shot a few months before in a dark night: two poets called Said Soltanpour and Rahman Hatefi.

Of course their names didn't appear in a single newspaper. No one was allowed to mourn for them, not even their families. They remained dishonoured under heavy black earth. And up to the present day no one may visit their graves. Perhaps they missed a letter of solidarity from you – a writer who a short time previously had been condemned to death by the same people?

Anyway: we, Mr Rushdie, those living colleagues, missed this "unique" opportunity to honour them with respect and gain worldwide public attention for their bitter fate.

Yes, that's it. That's what bothered me: that you push your own problem so much into the foreground and overlook the others who have the same problem. Many of your utterances give this impression, even when you connect them with the fate of others: "Today it's me. And if this campaign, these attacks which have to do with *The Satanic Verses* should be successful, it could be someone else tomorrow," you said in your latest interview, last week. That, unfortunately, is true. But there is another painful truth: namely that there are still eleven fellow-writers in the same situation today, as you must have read in the *Writers in Prison Report 91* made public at the PEN-Centre meeting of last October. Our colleague Anegelika Mechtel writes in this report that "the need to hide" appears often. "Here Salman Rushdie is not a unique case, the committee [of PEN for imprisoned writers] mentions eleven such cases in its statistics..." Further the report shows that 739 fellow-writers were persecuted last year in 75 countries. "323 of these are presently imprisoned in the prisons of their countries, as far as the committee is aware. The persecution of the other 416, apart from the above-mentioned prison sentences, often long-term, consists of the following: murder, kidnapping, murder threats, physical attacks, the need to hide, banning, expulsion..."

Mr Rushdie, I don't want to elaborate further on the miserable and depressing situation of our colleagues throughout the world, as this report paints it. A frightening picture of injustice, terror, violence and deprivation would emerge. You know all this, because you are yourself a victim of this injustice, this terror, of violence and deprivation.

Yes, your case is unique. Because the death sentence against you was pronounced by a foreign terrorist regime of which you are not a citizen. It is justly described as unique, but it can't have such a prominent place if at the same time at least 739 other, almost similar and terrible cases exist. I don't think the former chairman of Zaire's Writers Union is too bothered whether his death sentence was pronounced by a Zairean despot or a Kenyan one. After his successful escape from prison he still feels threatened and persecuted and is still fleeing, although he now lives in a "free" European country, in some kind of "security".

The same is true for the 33-year-old South Korean poet Park Ki-Pyong, sentenced to life imprisonment for "anarchist thinking". For those whose life is sought after and whose freedom is to be taken away it makes no difference whether the eyes of their judges, juries and executioners are blue or dark. They simply want, like you, to avoid losing their own "skin" for having engaged themselves through literature. Mr Rushdie, you once said: "Saving my skin. As if it was despicable to want something like that. It was depressing to find that people valued my skin so little." (*die tageszeitung*, 24 September 1991)

I value your "skin", Mr Rushdie, as well as the freedom to speak and to write. I value all my colleagues who have lost their "skin" because of that, and those who engage themselves to bring this obscene injustice and this unequal fight to an end. I especially value my unknown eleven colleagues to whom I will write an open letter immediately I have finished my letter of solidarity to you. An open letter – because I don't know where to find them under the skies of their homelands.

Greetings, your

Fahimeh Farsaie

José Saramago

Dear Salman Rushdie,

Often during those long drawn out three years during which you have hidden yourself from those who seek to murder you, I had to think that you, in contrast to those monks who left the world behind in order to be closer to God, had to leave the world behind in order to flee God. People have condemned you in the name of God, but much time has passed, and He (I use here the traditional way of writing) has not shown His agreement with the sentence, nor given a sign that He Himself is willing to carry out the sentence (since He is the Almighty One), and so I am entertaining some doubts as to what God has to do with this affair.

A God would not only be absurd, who lets people carry out sentences He Himself has not pronounced, these sentences having however been pronounced in order to defend Him, such a God would also be irresponsible; but God is by definition the being with the most responsibility of all beings (if we care to define it that way) who exist in the Universe. Since God did not pronounce this sentence against you, nor sign any proclamation to that effect, the whole matter is a crime committed by human beings against other human beings, a crime like all those other crimes of the past, which have been committed in His name, and certainly will continue to be committed in the future.

Dear Rushdie, you will allow me to make this comment: your conversion to Islam was useless, as useless as Galileo's recantation, since God, wherever He is, takes no notice of the little happenings amongst us human beings, even though millions of us have died in this world here below, because his identity carries with it so many different names and attributes.

You will have noticed that I have up to now avoided

speaking of all the usual things like freedom of speech and of expression, the holy respect for life, tolerance, forgiveness, of gossip and of evil deeds, crime and responsibility, and finally the fact that we are more or less conscious of all this, not to forget the social need for some general ethical values, which exist independently of authority, be it celestial or temporal.

I can imagine, dear Rushdie, that you are tired of reading or hearing these kind of things, and that is why I will tell you a small popular story, a short fable from my childhood, which has stayed with me during all my intervening years. I never thought that the story would one day be useful, especially not in such a serious situation, in a letter to you, which, being an open letter, can be ready by everybody, and only God knows what the readers will think, who may have totally different ideas about how one goes about expressing one's respect in a situation such as yours.

But let us turn to the story (The bread that we eat is made of stories), and the critics will be silent. Once upon a time there lived a man who beat his wife every day. She could be as careful, as obedient as she wanted, reading his wishes from his eyes, never raising her voice, not even saying, "this is my mouth". Her husband always found a pretext to beat her. Once, though, the poor woman had been so careful, that the man saw the evening hour draw near, and the time to go to bed, without having given her her daily punishment.

I forgot to say, dear Rushdie, that this story happened in a village in the country, during the hot summer. Our man had gotten so used to finding reasons when there were none, that he found a way out. He told his wife: "It is so hot, it would be better if we slept outside, in back of the house." He did not have to ask his wife twice, and quickly she had set the bed up in the small garden, and it was beautiful there under the wonderful canopy of stars, the whole sumptuous Milky Way.

The man lay down, the woman lay down, surprised that a day had gone by without her having been beaten, when her husband suddenly asked her: "Woman, what is that?" And she, full of innocence: "What?" And he: "All those stars in the sky, all over the sky." "But, husband, don't you know that that is the street of Santiago." Street of Santiago is what we Hispanics and Iberians, and Christians, call the Milky Way. Hardly had she finished speaking than her husband cried out: "What, you set my bed out on the street, where a car might fall down upon me?" And he set upon giving her the beating she had nearly missed getting that day.

I do not have to explain the moral of this story, dear Rushdie. Ten years ago I wrote a novel, which is still around: "If the Holy Office says so, all good reasons are bad and all bad reasons are good, and if there is a lack of this or that, then there are the tortures of water and fire, of rack and gallows, in order to call them forth from nothingness and from silence." That's how it is. We were never in God's hands, but we were always in the hands of might.

I do not know whether we will meet one day or whether you are condemned to perpetual isolation. Both the so-called international community and the opinion we call public try to do their best in forgetting you, since you are a bother for them, and are thinking about the problems our planet faces and what to do about them. I would not like to have to write to you again in a year, but I am afraid that is how it will be, because the craziness of this shitty world in which we live is so all-encompassing.

I embrace you,

José Saramago

Graham Swift

Dear Salman,

Three years have gone by and those who have defended you have learnt not to press too hard the special plea of literature. Literature is not the issue; the issue is your rights as a citizen. As a fellow writer, therefore, I should have no more nor less vital an interest in your plight than any other citizen of this country. Yet as a fellow writer it is easier for me (though it is still not easy) to imagine myself in your position; as a friend it is harder for me – impossible to turn you into some adaptable abstraction.

They have been many and monstrous, these abstract Salman Rushdies, born out of your enforced isolation; these concocted and distorted Salman Rushdies; these failures to remember that you are, after all, only a man. It has been painful to watch the man I know transformed by this party and that beyond all recognition.

The same for your book. The rich and complex work I have read and reread has become a mere vessel for received ideas, a contention, a notion, a supposition, a formula, at worst only a name the bare utterance of which is sufficient to cause storms of prejudice. So perhaps it is necessary after all, if only for accuracy's sake, to plead the cause of literature, which is ever against abstraction and on the side of flesh-and-blood complexity.

Nearly three years ago I wrote a letter to a British newspaper in which I made literature – distinguishing it from propaganda, dogma and the making of arguments and assertions – my principal rallying point in your defence. Perhaps that was naive and, in those early days, all too hopeful of me; but this is what I wrote then and I see no reason to alter it: "Propaganda is an instrument of power; art is an instrument of life. Whatever else *The Satanic Verses* is or does, it has life: energy, invention, colour, animation, intelligence, humour, questions, doubts, passion, quickness: life. There may be many arguing over the book who have not read it; but let those who have read it, whatever their view, acknowledge first that the book breathes what all human beings share, and let them argue from there."

It is easy to turn a man into what he is not if you do not happen to know him. It is easy to turn a book into what it is not if you have not truly read it. Three deplorable years have passed, but in this letter to you I would like to celebrate literature and honour your contribution to it. How scant the stock of literature would be if all the books that had occasioned offence had been excluded from it; if they had been denied for ever to those successions of readers who have granted them in the end the respect of humanity for humanity. How poor and mean a world that would so prescribe and proscribe.

I salute your courage, I send my love. Amid all ease that I wish you, I offer you this wish of a writer to a writer: may you have many, many and more and more readers.

Graham Swift

William Styron

As the third anniversary of Salman Rushdie's sentence approaches, there is a sense of frustration and helplessness, and one feels at a loss to do much more than to express one's firm and continuing solidarity with this grievously outraged man, along with the forlorn hope that somehow he will be relieved of the edict that has caused him such unique suffering. That there is little cause for optimism may be seen in the recent development in Egypt, where the novelist Alaa Hamed was sentenced by a Security Court to eight years in prison for writing a novel deemed blasphemous. Like Rushdie in the period before his own sentence from Teheran, Hamed has been threatened with death by religious extremists.

Because Egypt is liberal by Islamic standards, the message is all the more sinister; less tolerance for writers, especially in religious matters, would now seem to be established as the order of the day. Were this manifestation of fundamentalist orthodoxy confined only to Islam it would be alarming enough, but such fanaticism is making itself felt in seemingly unlikely places – the United States of America, for example, the bastion of human rights. It may be that the most useful way to commemorate the atrocity committed upon Rushdie is to allow it to mirror similar attempts, made in the name of a Higher Power, to inflict mortal wounds on freedom.

Christians can be as prone as Muslims to narrow views. Former President Jimmy Carter, a "born-again" Christian, is a man rightfully admired by many for his humane and enlightened attitudes. Yet although he drew short of approving Rushdie's death sentence, he did express his philosophical accord with the Ayatollah's condemnation of the writer's alleged blasphemy. It would appear that when it comes to scriptural matters, Islamic or Christian, strict fundamentalists are kindred spirits. If such intolerance makes one thankful that the United States never evolved into a Christian theocracy, as Iran evolved into an Islamic one, it is also a reminder that religious bigotry is still a powerful force in American life.

Fortunately, this bigotry does not as yet affect writers, at least on an official level; as regards writers and written expression, the United States remains perhaps the freest nation on earth. But disastrous inroads are already being made upon human rights by religious extremists, and the chief area of strife is that of abortion. While virtually every advanced nation has successfully dealt with this matter, permitting abortion – this includes Catholic countries like France and Italy – in the United States the issue has become one of hate-filled conflict. Its failure of resolution has strained if not perverted our laws and our political process, and torn at the fabric of society. And it is a society in which every poll has indicated that the overwhelming majority of the people favour women's right to obtain an abortion if they so wish. The obstacles to such rights have been put in place most effectively not by those who oppose abortion on reasonable philosophical or personal grounds – yet who deem it improper for the state to interfere with a woman's decision – but by the forces of religious fanaticism.

One could superimpose the hysterical faces of the mob of recent anti-abortion demonstrators in Wichita, Kansas, upon the faces of the true believers in Bradford, England, who several years ago were calling for Rushdie's blood, and the faces would merge into sameness. Both the Islamic extremists and the American anti-abortion zealots (ironically termed "pro-life"), who are composed primarily of Protestant fundamentalists and Catholics of the far right, wish to achieve the same level of obliteration: to obliterate a man's life, and to obliterate a woman's right to determine a central aspect of her destiny – childbirth. Each group would claim the authority to abrogate ultimate human freedoms – an aim that is fascistic – and each would not shrink from the violence that is intolerable to civilized society. The frightening and ruthless passion each group has demonstrated in pursuing its goals has made it clear that such fanaticism is

ecumenical in scope, not only an Eastern phenomenon but
one that threatens the West as well.

On this anniversary of the beginning of Salman Rushdie's
ordeal it may be of small consolation to the man himself to
say that his living martyrdom, if such it may be called, has
allowed the world to perceive more clearly the dangers and
terrors that blind orthodoxy poses to man and woman
everywhere.

William Styron

Dermot Bolger

Dear Salman Rushdie,

I am taking the liberty of writing to you as a fellow novelist, although it is unlikely that you will ever have heard of me. For my part, even if I were not an author, it is virtually impossible that I would not know both your name and the title of one of your novels, *The Satanic Verses*. Few writers can ever have received such fame, and ironically, in a world where agents and publishers are perpetually initiating publicity campaigns, few writers can ever have wanted it less.

Visiting my neighbouring island, it is not your absence I keep encountering but your invisible presence. Any caller to the publishers we share becomes immediately aware of you when confronted with body searches at the door, when asked to put their briefcases through a scanning machine, when forced to wear numbered identity tags around their necks and allowed to go nowhere in the building without a minder.

On my last reading in London, in Waterstones in Hampstead, the staff were still recovering from the day when you suddenly appeared there and sat quietly signing copies of your children's book for amazed customers before vanishing again into the limbo which constitutes your present life.

Tomorrow, Valentine's Day, is the third anniversary of the *fatwa* against you in particular and those involved in the publication of your novel in general, the third anniversary of your disappearance into a life which we can only begin to try and imagine. I don't mean just the physical details of safe houses and armed guards, but the mental world of that confinement.

We in Ireland have had our innocent prisoners, the Birmingham Six in prison cells in Britain, Nicky Kelly in a jail of our own, Brian Keenan naked and chained in a darkened room in Beirut. All situations where the physical conditions are worse than your own, but even with Keenan, caught up by chance in a situation we could barely comprehend and unheard of for so long that he might have been dead, we could imagine an end to his torment. For him a day came when the curse was lifted, when he arrived at Dublin airport into a virtual wall of love. For the Birmingham Six the dream could sustain them that one day they would emerge victorious from a courtroom with arms raised and the possibility of somehow rebuilding their lives.

A writer thinks and writes between the lines of official laws and stances. You are too intelligent to believe that such a black-and-white moment can ever occur for you. Even should the death threat and the sick bounty offered on your life be revoked tomorrow by a more liberal Iranian government, your freedom could not be guaranteed. You would simply become an even more potent symbol for fundamentalists, no longer just caught between hardline Islam and the world, but now a pawn in a struggle between rival factions of fundamentalism.

Tomorrow night in Dublin, as in cities all over the world, your fellow writers will gather to protest for your right and our rights to the freedom of expression. Because your struggle, bizarre and inflated far beyond the realms of fiction, is all our struggles, is the struggle of the writer and the artist and the individual to steer his or her own course against those myriad forces which take many shapes and forms of self-righteousness, but are all bent on creating their own versions of conformity.

I know that you would not wish to see yourself set up as yet another symbol of anything, that your problems have been created not by people who have read your work but by those who wish to use it for their own purposes. However, while it is easy for us to be incredulous at the primeval barbarism of your self-appointed judges, within our own societies – as our old structures crumble away – there are increasingly dangerous forces striving to impose new "liberal" conformities.

Compared to the outrageous treatment, which both you and others involved in *The Satanic Verses* have received, the pressures on contemporary writers to conform may seem slight. Yet while your jurors are seen for what they are, the modern "liberal" forces are more subtle and insidious. They would see themselves as literate and reasoned and generally "in favour" of the artist, as defenders of the rights of "oppressed" groups as against oppressors of the rights of an individual.

It would be interesting to test this liberalism by reshaping *The Satanic Verses* to be a novel about gays or American blacks, or switching the religious icons – to make them as offensive to many of us as *The Satanic Verses* is to many decent ordinary Muslims – by having Mary, the mother of God, her mother's sister, Mary the wife of Ceopas, and Mary Magdalene portrayed as prostitutes hovering at the foot of the cross. None would sentence you to death but it would be fun watching them run for cover.

No doubt there have been many times when you wished you had never begun that book. However, I suspect that the detached part of you which is instinctively pure writer would not change a word of it. You may have been one of the few people involved in its publication who really understood the assault on fundamentalism which you were creating. On my birthday last week I mentioned jokingly to a number of people in British publishing that I had attained the age of Christ and each of them had to ask what age Christ had been. Without even a basic knowledge of Christianity what hope had they of grasping the impact of your work on Muslims?

I suspect the West has grown very tired of you. In the world of ever-changing political alignments, where collective amnesia is an everyday wonder and villains are only villains until they are allies, your book, like all good literature, juts out like a bad conscience. For the media, any war which drags on for too long ceases to sustain interest. We like stories which can be tied up quickly. *The Satanic Verses* is not one of them. Few of those who have read it can have understood what it was about, few of those who would understand it will have deemed it fit to read. The argument is no longer about the book's merits or faults or about literature;

the contents of the book have been lost in a war between times and exploding and receding cultures.

I strongly urge my government to put pressure on Iran to lift the appalling and sick *fatwa* against you (which has already claimed lives), but you should not hold your breath. The cow may be sacred in your native land, but the selling of them is sacred in mine. For a nation which struggled so bravely for independence, it has shown in recent years a marked lack of independence. The sight of the Dalai Lama being shunned by government ministers here last year for fear of offending greater powers is one which filled many citizens of this small nation with shame. Let me say that, for me, nothing which is outside the range of human experience can be outside the scope of the writer to explore. *The Satanic Verses* is a work of blasphemy and many people have a right to be offended by its contents. Based upon *The Gay News* verdict of some years back, I have no doubt that there would have been a strong campaign to ban it in Britain should its targets have been Christian. Yet when any religion is hijacked in the name of love, when any religious leader invokes the name of God to send barefoot children walking through minefields, no more than when any Western leader calls God's blessing down on genocide, a far greater blasphemy takes place; a blasphemy which calls out to be redeemed by smashing those very icons which have been invoked. As Pier Paolo Pasolini told the Radical Party Congress, the writer must "continue, unafraid, obstinate, eternally contrary; to demand, to will, to identify yourself with all that is different – to scandalize and blaspheme."

They may have taken away your liberty, Mr Rushdie, but they have not taken away your voice. My wish for you is that you may continue to work and you should know that tomorrow night there are many writers in Ireland, as all over the world, gathered in your name to proclaim their belief in your right to speak.

Yours sincerely,

Dermot Bolger

Norman Mailer

Dear Salman Rushdie,

I have thought of you often over the last few years. Many of us begin writing with the inner temerity that if we keep searching for the most dangerous of our voices, why then, sooner or later we will outrage something fundamental in the world, and our lives will be in danger. That is what I thought when I started out, and so have many others, but you, however, are the only one of us who gave proof that this intimation was not ungrounded. Now you live in what must be a living prison of contained paranoia, and the toughening of the will is imperative, no matter the cost to the poetry in yourself. It is no happy position for a serious and talented writer to become a living martyr. One does not need that. It is hard enough to write at one's best without bearing a hundred pounds on one's back each day, but such is your condition, and if I were a man who believed that prayer was productive of results, I might wish to send some sort of vigour and encouragement to you, for if you can transcend this situation, more difficult than any of us have known, if you can come up with a major piece of literary work, then you will rejuvenate all of us, and literature, to that degree, will flower.

So, my best to you, old man, wherever you are ensconsed, and may the muses embrace you.

Cheers,

Norman Mailer

Elfriede Jelinek

Dear Salman Rushdie,

What does one say to another who must stay where he is, who is no longer master of his fate? One who writes – therefore whose thoughts are meant to endure. Thoughts that go beyond the writer, though he himself must remain in his secret place. He who creates something enduring should be allowed to choose where and how he rests. You are not allowed that. You were torn away and forced to be always somewhere else, and probably never where you would have preferred to remain.

That is a tragedy difficult for the bystander to imagine. You have professed belonging to Islam, the Islam which decrees the veil for women such as myself. Which forbids them to be present, to be seen. But women who feel that they belong to Islam say that they must not be seen, although they themselves can see. That gives them power: to be able to see without being seen. They are, and they are not, and thus they have the right of the unseen eye. I do not know to what degree your right to see is restricted. Your right to remain certainly is. What remains to us? We, your colleagues who are not threatened, we must fight for your homecoming, which for the poet is always a coming home to one's self. Yet *that* homecoming none can deny you; because that which is your own remains to you – your thought and your writing. That is all that remains to you. Maybe that is not enough. Certainly you need a homecoming that is also a going out, a going out into the most unfamiliar, perhaps a going out that must needs be into the most strange? Into the eye of the hurricane. Into the roaring mouths. Into the memorials running with blood.

What does one say to another who is forced into a hidden

life and who still professes that religion which forces him to that hiding, moreover under the constant threat of death? Of course it's your right to think so. What colonial arrogance could possibly censure you? And what colonial arrogance could censure you for heaping ridicule on what you obviously hold sacred? (For you have always denied being blasphemous.) The British-Pakistani author/filmmaker Hanif Kureishi says: "I would find it impertinent and condescending to spare my Asiatic figures the satire, mockery and parody to which I subject my white characters." Arrogant and patronizing is any attempt to spare literary protagonists the sharp vision of irony – indeed, why not? of absurdity – only because they come from a culture that is not Western. Such a sparing would be a denial. From the standpoint of the master it would deny something precisely to those to whom in the first world of the white man all else is equally denied.

Nevertheless: I don't know what I should say to you. That we all belong together, we who, in writing, are at home with ourselves? That would be presumptuous, because I may go wherever and whenever I will. That we can only be at home when we fight our way through the foreign – the strangeness, actually – with the blunt knives of our language, in order to become one with what we write about? In order, at the end and finally, to remain where we thus arrive? But I fear that even that place is insecure; scarcely arrived, we shall want to go forth again.

Are you denied history, which itself is the process of becoming at home somewhere only to break out of that home once again? Are you forced to an absolute standstill?

No. The path of history leads directly to you and then beyond you. And you are in fact the fastest among us, because you know that you will never learn, never know the truth, whose glib borrowers constantly divide it among themselves (those smeared scraps!) without ever diminishing it. The truth that like bloody flesh is torn out of the critical course of history by the thousands of stretched fists in the sea of screaming fanatics. But history moves ever onward. And you, Salman Rushdie, you do, too. With only a few friends by your side, the path will become wider, and, sometime, you will arrive.

Warmly, your

Elfriede Jelinek

Kazuo Ishiguro

Dear Mr Rushdie,

Before boarding a train from Scotland back to London recently, I came across one of your novels, *The Satanic Verses*, at the railway station kiosk and bought it to read on the long train journey. I soon found myself engrossed – the journey went by very quickly – and on arriving home I continued to read it right through to the end. I thought you wouldn't mind my taking this opportunity to tell you how much I enjoyed the novel and of the deep impression it has made on me.

The longing for love, the warring forces within one who both embraces and rejects his origins, the search for moral parameters in a world of chaos and flux – all these things I found marvelously expressed through the novel's many diverse characters. And I am sure I am not the first to have felt at the heart of the novel, for all its exuberance and noise, a profound sense of loneliness – the sort of loneliness experienced in the middle of a crowd. Having myself settled in a country other than the one of my birth, I could identify with many of your characters' feelings. However – I was born in Japan – I was not familiar with the particular hue of emotions deriving from the old colonial relationship between Britain and India; your moving portrayal of your Indian characters' struggle for a sense of themselves has, I feel, led me to an insight and a feeling of sympathy for which I was previously not equipped.

I have a good friend – a Chinese now living in Canada – with whom I have long conversations concerning his deeply mixed feelings towards his "home" culture. His relationship with his father came very much to my mind while following the troubled relationship at the centre of your book between Saladin and his father. I am sure my friend would find this portrait very affecting, and I would without hesitation send him a copy of the book were it not that his father is now gravely ill and I fear the extremely moving death scene at the close of the novel might be rather too upsetting. So perhaps I will not send him the book for the moment. But in this age of migration and "multi-cultural-ism", there must be countless others around this globe who will discover in your book a valuable exploration of their hopes and sadnesses.

I have to confess that prior to last week's train journey I had not read any of your works, but now I will certainly seek out all your other books. I will be interested to know if these also concern themselves with the themes of cultural identity and the longing for love. I will also look forward to your future novels with much interest.

I am myself a writer and if you ever happen to be passing through my part of London, I would very much welcome the chance to meet and talk with you – perhaps over a beer or a coffee. (Our neighbourhood has a number of fine cafés which I feel you would enjoy.) But I expect you are a busy man, so I will not hold out too much hope on this score. I just wanted to thank you for the experience of *The Satanic Verses*. This may be a cliché, but it is true: novels like yours have helped me learn a little more of what it means to be human.

Yours sincerely,

Kazuo Ishiguro

Johannes Mario Simmel

Dear Mr Salman Rushdie,

This letter is an attempt to bring you some comfort and tell you the real reason for the terrible situation you are in. Namely: in writing your book you have interfered with the play of the primal forces of nature.

A friend of mine, an American economist, explained this to me when we spoke about it a few days ago.

You, Mr Rushdie, said my American friend, are a great writer, an idealistic dreamer, who still thinks in terms of nations, ideologies, gods, freedom from fear and misery, freedom of speech and of religion, democracy, justice and human rights. There are, however (said my American friend), no longer any nations, countries, ideologies, nor are there freedom, democracy, human rights, East and West, nor a Third World, nor God.

There are Higher Things!

Meaning one huge, enormous, incredibly interwoven, reciprocally influencing, multi-faceted and multi-national system of companies, like IBM and ITT, Union Carbide and MBB, Thyssen and Exxon. And this system adheres to the immutable laws of economics. The world, dear Mr Rushdie, is a department store; the world, dear Mr Rushdie, is business. And with your book you disturbed this business – only for a moment, of course.

Let me explain how this applies to the German (not the international) business world, since I am more familiar with the German situation.

The disruption you provoked had to be ended as quickly as possible. That is clear. Already on July 1 of last year, the news agency AFP reported – I am not making anything up, only citing facts – that the German Economics Minister, Jürgen Möllemann, was in Tehran (where the Ayatollah Khomeini had sentenced you to death because of your book *The Satanic Verses*) for discussions on the improvement of

German-Iranian economic relations. The Federal Republic, so says the report, is Iran's most important trading partner, and Iran, in turn, is the largest importer of German goods in the Near East. Mr Möllemann was accompanied by a group of German businessmen and industrialists, who represented 35 German firms. In diplomatic circles it was said that there would be unlimited loan guarantees for exports extended through the Hermes company in Bonn, since the German government had lifted the previous ceiling of five hundred million dollars.

Together with other governments, the German government really did everything possible to eliminate the disturbance you brought to the department-store world. Experts were counting on an increase in bilateral trade from 4.6 billion dollars in 1990 to 6 billion in 1991.

In the face of this pleasant increase, the successors of the Ayatollah Khomeini also increased the price on your head to 4.5 million dollars. And since Mr Möllemann's negotiations were so successfully concluded (also in July 1991), the Italian translator of your supposedly blasphemous *Verses* was stabbed and your Japanese translator in Tokyo was murdered. You are beginning to understand, Mr Rushdie, that the world is a business.

And what a business.

In February 1991 (by which time you had been living underground, hidden by the police, for two years) Foreign Minister Genscher discussed with his Iranian colleague the possibility of cultural exchanges. His Ministry had informed the head of the Book Fair, Mr Weidhaas, that the boycott of Iranian publishers which had been in effect since the call for your murder was not conducive to flourishing trade relations. As a consequence, dear Mr Rushdie, Mr Weidhaas and the officials of the Book Fair decided to lift the boycott, and they invited eight Iranian publishers to the 1991 Fair.

As early as April a group from Bonn, including Mr Barthold C. Witte, Cultural Director of the Foreign Office, travelled to Tehran. Mr Weidhaas also flew along. An "Iranian Cultural Festival" was planned for Düsseldorf, which would be organized by the city of Düsseldorf, the

Tehran Office of Islamic Affairs, and – something is missing! – by the Thyssen trade representative. Aha, there it is!

The cultural program took place in September 1991. It included events like "Music from Tabriz" and "Classical Music of Tehran." The Book Fair was scheduled to be held right afterwards, from October 9 to 14. The press had criticized Mr Peter Weidhaas for inviting eight Iranian publishers. (*Die Zeit*: "Shame on a book fair which in this manner actually betrays the writer Rushdie, who has to fear for his life." *Die Frankfurter Allgemeine Zeitung*: "The book fair's breach of faith is a big boost for the fundamentalists, who are deeply convinced of Western weakness." *Die taz*: "Business as usual.")

Mr Weidhaas, however: "We are not able to review our decision... We are not a" – not a department store? But no! – "not an institution that is concerned with moral questions, and we are not censors. Rather, our duty is to gather together all the countries of the world at this book fair."

Mr Weidhaas, who had taken the recommendation of the Foreign Office so to heart, did see a way to review the situation, namely when big American and German publishing houses protested in outrage, saying they would not come to the Book Fair. Then Mr Weidhaas – according to an AP report of 26 September (remember, the Düsseldorf "Iranian Cultural Festival" had been set for September) – disinvited the eight Iranian publishers he had originally invited, in order, as was explained, "to ensure the viability of the 1991 Book Fair".

And what can we once again learn from this, Mr Rushdie?

Once again, we can learn that literature and all the other fine arts are only fig leaves behind which this raw world can (sort of) conceal its business dealings.

It would be only human, dear Mr Rushdie, if you, who has to fear being murdered at any moment, would say: whether fig leaf or persecuted writer, that is all of no consequence. What was and is being done to me is a crime, and somebody should finally do something about it, decisively, so that after all this time underground I can finally live again in peace and safety.

True enough, Mr Rushdie. However, you really should not only think of yourself. You see, in August 1991 – only one example – German banks (covered to the last penny by Hermes securities, according to a DPA report of August 13) lent Iran a half billion Marks, which was to finance the construction, modernization and expansion of petrochemical projects. What, dear Mr Rushdie, if *because of you* Iran had not taken the half billion? Oh, and just think of the numerous German-Iranian projects that are part of Tehran's five-year plan. We deliver so much...

We have, of course, extremely strict trade regulations, but it's like with the white queen in *Alice in Wonderland*: first she screams loudly, and then she pricks herself. First our heroic industrialists deliver poison gas and gas factories to Libya, to Iraq, and to many other interested parties, and only then does Bonn threaten *even* stricter export regulations. German companies have sent Tornado fighter planes to Israel's neighbour Jordan, nuclear plants or their main components to Iraq, India, Pakistan, and so on. Basic components of the "Scud" rockets went to Iraq, from where they were launched towards Israel during the Gulf War; weapons are sent everywhere where they are in demand, and they are in demand everywhere.

What is the reason for all this, Mr Rushdie? Pure profit motive? Never! All of this occurs because of social reasons! So that *jobs* don't get lost! Dear Mr Rushdie, you can count on the sympathy of all Western economic leaders, but, please think of this: with you, at worst only *your* job would be lost. If we, and the Americans and the French, and so many others, were to stop doing business with Iran because of you, how many jobs would *then* be lost? Hundreds of thousands, Mr Rushdie, many hundreds of thousands! You can see that, can't you? Common interest before self-interest, goes a German proverb. And so the circle is closed.

With your book you have interfered with the primal forces of nature, said my American friend. You should have written a book about the world as a business! Nothing, absolutely nothing, would have happened to you! You see how these gentlemen do their jobs – responsibly, proudly, in full public view, and with shoulders held high. This book, Mr Rushdie, this book – and everything would have been fine.

Sincerely,

Johannes Mario Simmel

P.S. I have just read what I have written, and I feel terrible. What I just said isn't true! A book about the world as a department store would have caused the same people to condemn you for *political* blasphemy, and would have had the same fate. I beg your pardon, Mr Rushdie, I beg your pardon! I wanted to comfort you. Now I see how poorly I went about it. But why? Maybe because there is no comfort?

Ralph Giordano

My dear esteemed Salman Rushdie,

"What lies beyond there? Hell!"

And with that the pure "Aryan" German who hid my family warned me when my Jewish mother was threatened with deportation, knowing full well that discovery by the Gestapo meant not only our, but also their death. They hid us nevertheless.

Hell: that was a lightless dungeon behind a narrow passageway, an extension of the former laundry of a phosphorescently glowing house amidst a landscape of ruins, three-quarters destroyed by bombs, in the north of Hamburg. "Hell" was a hole in the cellar, in standing water, cold, where the walls oozed wet, among rats. Though the rats, eventually, adjusted to our presence, quite visibly in fact, we did not adjust to theirs, nor to their ever more daring attempts to get a bite of us as we were steadily weakening. "Hell" was months of mortal fear, day and night; it was utter gloom, frost, hunger and the absolute silence of those who were hiding. For all around the extension of our brave hostess's former laundry the neighbours were burrowed in what remained of the cellars in that landscape of ruins, and we dared not let them know of our existence... When we five – father, mother, and three sons – finally crawled out of the inferno in the early morning of 4 May 1945, we hardly resembled human beings – but we were free.

What I mean to say in retelling this memory is: first, that I know what it means to have to hide to save your life. And second, that I can imagine the difference between a situation like the one we lived in then, in which one can hope for an end to the terror, and one which threatens to last a "lifetime", as in your case. But I do not want to accept a more merciful fate for myself than your persecutors plan for you, Salman Rushdie. I want a "May 4th" for you, too, and as fast as possible.

Everything we can do, everything that can be done from the outside, must aim for the repeal of the judgement – "valid until the end of history" – that the Islamic fundamentalists under Iranian leadership are supposed to have handed down. For all who wish to help, wherever they may be on this globe, but above all for those of us who are writers, the highest maxim must be: don't be intimidated! Who dares to presume the prerogative over life and death? And who will be the next victim? The avalanche of the self-proclaimed religious "Anti-Enlightenment" that was set off by the Ayatollah Khomeini can, today or tomorrow, bury anyone alive who dares to publicly defy the demon of The Only True Intolerance. Our freedom to live, to think, to speak and to write what and how we like – this most precious of all attainments shall become dependent on behaviour acceptable to the orchestrators of an Islamic fundamentalism that has long since advanced from worldwide annoyance to worldwide threat? It must be defied, now! Of course, this is a demand to politicians to enforce the primacy of human rights and to break that of the economy. Calling for your murder, Salman Rushdie, have been representatives of governments with which the democracies of this world, among them Germany, have the best of relations, not to mention multi-billion dollar sales of weapons. Are the presidents, chancellors and ministers of the powerful nations of this earth not satisfied with the murder of the Japanese, the injury of the Italian translator of your book? Nor with the killing of the Turkish author Turan Dursun, felled by seven bullets? And did not Radio Tehran celebrate that cowardly assassination in September 1990, with a victory announcement? – "In his works Turan Dursun betrayed the holy Islamic religion and defamed the prophet Muhammad." What of this is true? Nothing. Our Turkish colleague, a publicist and mufti, was an enlightened Muslim who was well-versed in the Koran – and a critic of fundamentalist orthodoxy. For that he had to die.

"When," I ask my government, "when will you do something in the 'Salman Rushdie case'?" Yes, when will one part ways with the national collective of notorious pacifists who lose their will to action as soon as they are faced with a moral crisis? We must keep after the politicians in the "matter of Salman Rushdie". But above all we writers must mobilize ourselves. Let us offer enduring resistance to the fundamentalist attack and oppose the small in spirit – not the least those in our own ranks – to whom nothing else occurs but the all-too familiar "there is really nothing one can do..."

But indeed there is – *with the power of the word!*

In closing, a short historical note:

On 13 October 1761, one Marc Antoine Calas, 28 years old and son of the draper Jean Calas, hanged himself in the attic of his parents' home in Toulouse. There was no doubt that it was a suicide, even though his motive remained a puzzle to his inconsolable family. But the year 1761 was also the eighteenth year of the reign of His Most Catholic Majesty, Louis XV, and the Calas were Huguenots, adherents of French Protestantism, a weakened Church, but still embodying a socio-economic power feared by the absolutist monarchy nearly two centuries after the Massacre of St Bartholomew. So Jean Calas was charged with murdering his son in order to prevent his intended conversion. The court records of the interrogation in this capital case are known. They prove that Jean Calas was unshakeable in maintaining his innocence. Nevertheless, the judgment was "Guilty!" Before the criminal was sent to the stake, the judge of Toulouse turned him over for "standard" and "special" torture – the Roman Church intended to get the heretic's confession. They didn't.

The execution occurs on 9 March 1762, and it exposes the gruesome character of a justice system dependent upon the clergy: bound naked on a wheel, head down, the arms and legs of Jean Calas are broken with a heavy iron bar, each limb in two places, at intervals calculated to prolong his agony, while a priest holds a cross to the face of the man for him to kiss, but he turns his head away. Then, finally, the executioner gives him the fatal blow, shattering his ribcage with the thick end of the bar. Thus died Jean Calas – it lasted two hours.

But the story doesn't end there. Voltaire, the "conscience of his age", learns of the judicial murder only after the execution. He investigates for a long time before writing on 13 February 1763, "I dare to be as sure of Calas's innocence as I am of my own existence." Then the great enlightener mobilizes the whole of his influence in Europe tirelessly for over two years. The decisive moment is the publication in 1764 of his *Treatise on Tolerance*, an exhaustive study of the effects of intolerance, written in the clear prose of a convinced humanist. It leads to the reopening of the case, which, on 9 March 1765, results in a new judgement: "Innocent!" The unbelievable, unexpected revocation – it could not bring Jean Calas back to life. But the authorities, with their self-righteousness and their lies, were defeated this time – through the power of the word! Victor Hugo, on the 100th anniversary of Voltaire's death on 30 May 1878, before his sarcophagus in the Paris Pantheon: "You argued *against* the tyrants and the beast, and *for* the cause of the human race, and you won. Great man, may you be blessed forever!"

May you, Salman Rushdie, triumph still a living man. The power of the word will contribute to this effort. Modern communications technology has given us writers and journalists the means for this as never before.

The Menetekel written on the wall of the outgoing century against its tyrants, despots, dictators, torturers and "monopolists of the truth", the mortal enemy which political, ideological and religious criminals will never accept, is called: public opinion! We will use it. That is a pledge.

In this spirit, Salman Rushdie, I honour you, and in solidarity I greet you!

Unswervingly, your

Ralph Giordano

Pierre Guyotat

Dear Salman Rushdie,

The Infidel that I am respects your original religion as lovingly as I respect my own, Catholicism.

You continue courageously to live under a decree that is imposing, foolish, cowardly, and sacrilegious.

The flash of the eye of God Allah seeks you in England and throughout the world; it will illuminate you for your assassins, armed with machine guns, or knives, or Muhammad's noose.

One must really be a fool to take away your right to life, without trial, in front of the whole world, with great gestures of beard and robe; and without reflecting upon oneself, fornicator murderer of fornicators, old man murderer of children, polygamist stoner of women; to admit to the whole world that Islam must pay its Ravaillacs in the currency of the Great Satan.

Why didn't Ayatollah Khomeini go after you and kill you himself?

The eminent sage of Qum and Eeauphle – "*Certain among you live/to decrepitude/so that after having learned something/you know nothing at all*" – might he have taken himself for the subject of his long and weighty study, for God himself?

You know now what a so-called Sacred Scripture is, for it's that sacredness that is striking you. What is the more sacred, that is, the more credible: your writings, signed by you, corrected by you, under contract, published under your name; or these words which come to us from so far away, ravenous words, assumptionary words, repeated, rambling, outside, inside, in the day, at night, after drinking, on the back of a camel, a horse, a donkey, in the odour of women, of virgins, of young boys, and, after having been sifted by conclaves of the just, but also by liars, erected as

immutable divine revelation?
"When you read the Koran,
Beg God's protection
Against the cursed Demon"
(Koran. *Sura* of the Bees, near the *Fatwa*-verses).

The tenderness of faith, its rites (the washing of the feet on Holy Thursday), its holy places (the Tomb of the Summary marabout), its servants (the nomad, not the mass, prostrated toward the East, with hands which receive the world and give it back), its force of universal attraction: what have these priests and mullahs done with it everywhere? Crime and morals.

What can be done for you, Salman Rushdie, who has done his duty in prolonging the Koran, like others of us prolong the two Testaments? (Let us continue, let us wander, without pretension, let us add to the disorder of this world.)

Should those writers of Muslim origin, in various countries, gather together and compose a great Book of Verses as Satanic as possible?

As to we who live in the West, are we able today to offer you Space, so that you may write there, far from Earth?

I salute you, Salman Rushdie.

Pierre Guyotat

Translated by Professor Warren Motte

Avraham B. Yehoshua

Dear Salman Rushdie,

It must seem wholly natural (and even inevitable) to you to receive a letter of encouragement and solidarity from an Israeli writer. Just as he decreed a personal *fatwa* against you, the Ayatollah cast a collective *fatwa* against all we Israelis, calling on all the Muslims in the world to fight the holy war until Israel disappears from the face of the earth.

Obviously, you say, collective danger is not the same as the one that threatens an isolated individual. From the psychological point of view, at least, you are right. Our history, however, has shown us that threats against a people are not less dangerous and deadly than those directed against an individual. The members of a collectivity are supposed to protect each other, and yet each person therein exposes the group and draws it toward its common destiny.

My colleagues, the respectable writers from many countries who responded to the initiative inviting them to write letters of support to alert public opinion and to stop the obscene outrage of this death threat, have expressed their ideas and positions warmly and forcefully. I don't have a great deal to add to that which they have already said so pertinently. One might, however, remark that, if during a meeting of the European Council a simple resolution had been adopted, stating an ultimatum to Iran for the annulment of its deadly *fatwa* against you, threatening to break off all diplomatic relations, that might, I think, have ended this nightmare which is contrary to all the traditions of the spirit of Islam, a religion that has known wonderful periods of cultural and spiritual tolerance, as much for the Muslims as for the Christians and Jews that it sheltered.

How many more years must pass before men of state and politicans understand that a case like yours, in spite of your literary singularity, has become a textbook case which,

93

through indifference and silent complicity, will soon be transformed into a more and more deadly virus?

Until those governments wake up, I would like simply to encourage you in these difficult times that you are experiencing. Allow me simply to tell you this: in spite of the almost comic absurdity of your situation – and I use the word "comic" in the fantastic dimension that you have so often given it in your books – you restore to the literature in this end of the twentieth century a level of seriousness and responsibility that it had lost, I think, since the end of the Second World War.

Sometimes we write words that are different and strong, complex, painful words, words that people read with pleasure, laughter, or astonishment; but those people always consider our work as a sort of pastime, a sophisticated pastime perhaps, but a pastime nonetheless.

The death threat coming from Tehran in reaction to words, sentences, and descriptions, shows us that there are still people who take literature seriously. Imaginary descriptions seem to them to reflect something real; and the writer behind those descriptions seems to be responsible.

I hope with all my heart that this nightmare will end soon. With your "Iranian" story, however, you have restored to the literature of the last frivolous years of this century, so suddenly frightening, a sense of seriousness that we had thought long lost. For, truthfully, literature should also be a dangerous thing, a thing that speaks the truth, and its writers, men and women, should accept all its risks and all its responsibilities.

Yes, Salman Rushdie, from the depths of the terrible situation you find yourself in, from the depths of your suffering, you deserve some comfort in the thought that you have restored to all of us a certain sense of gravity.

To you!

Avraham B. Yehoshua

Translated by Professor Warren Motte

Mario Vargas Llosa

Dear Salman Rushdie,

Who would have ever guessed that Saturday afternoon when we went to a soccer game – the one we lost and ended up in a section of rowdy fans who sang something similar to "La Cucaracha" and threw their hats at the police – that later circumstances would make you the most celebrated contemporary victim of that extreme form of violence that is called religious fanaticism.

I am sure that I told you that afternoon or some other time the story of that colleague of mine at King's College with whom we coincided at times for lunch in a pub in the Strand. He was a well-read man, a good conversationalist, and had the appearance of being civilized. Until one day I heard him defend with cold conviction, in the name of tradition and culture – that dangerous thing that is called a people's "identity" – the practice of clipping a little girl's clitoris in order to assure her future temperance.

One of the truths that remains safe and sound in these times of hurricanes that level everything is the following: civilization is a very delicate film that can break with the first encounter with the demons of faith, disintegrate with the first assault of social injustice. These demons are running free over there where they proclaimed the *fatwa* against you and in the country I am from, where other types of fanatics have proposed constructing universal happiness by imposing terror, and in this Europe, where so many extraordinary things have happened recently that could be interpreted as a victory for good sense and rationality over lies and dogma. It has not been that way. And you – living on the run so that the hatred of that pack of dogs does not catch up to you – are there to break any illusion and to remind us that the battle has not been won and never will be won.

Now in this Germany reunited in democracy thanks to a formidable leap toward freedom by the people of East Germany, groups of savage skinheads run around hunting Turks and singing old racist tunes. In the France of the Declaration of Human Rights, respectable politicians on the left and on the right favour the ideas of the National Front, because, apparently, xenophobia and patriotism now win votes. In Ireland, in Spain, other patriots pulverize innocent citizens with dynamite in order to make abstract demonstrations. In countries where the culture of tolerance, pluralism and freedom seemed most deeply rooted – and in recent years all the hopes of the millions of people of the East intent on imitating their model – we notice symptoms of the old watch-tower spirit that seemed buried.

This return to tribal society, more specifically, closing oneself to one's own culture, beliefs and habits, closing one's eyes and ears to others, is not an unusual reaction before the rapid process of internationalization of life that the world, especially the Western world, lives. It is a defensive move against the unknown and against the formidable challenges that propose the possibility of a planet in which the development of freedoms has been eroding the borders, making them increasingly artificial and useless. But if this process is frustrated by the retrograde forces that are opposed to it, humanity will have taken a pitiful leap backwards, when it seemed better equipped than ever to move forward in the domestication of its demons.

We should not allow a complicitory silence to fall over the persecution of which you are victim nor that the public become accustomed to what is happening to you. It is our obligation as writers, for moral and practical reasons – for in a world where blackmail silences writers, literature could not exist – to maintain our indignation and protest alive. Remembering that this is an intolerable injustice and demanding that governments and public opinion mobilize until it ends. In very few cases, such as the one you are living, can we distinguish so clearly the line – often shady and wiggly – that divides the rational from the irrational, the just from the unjust, the barbarous from the civilized.

We will go to a soccer game again and we will learn to sing "La Cucaracha", my dear Salman.

Mario Vargas Llosa

Translated by Professor Raymond Williams

Andrzej Szczypiorski

Dear Mr Rushdie, dear colleague,

Three years ago, towards the beginning of 1989, I experienced a solemn occasion. In Vienna I was awarded the Austrian state medal for European literature. Just a few months before, after a few years of enforced silence, I had appeared once again as a writer for the readers in my fatherland. But in Poland I remained a citizen who made the authorities most uncomfortable. With effort I obtained a passport valid to leave Poland for Vienna. The official Polish representatives did not participate in the award ceremonies in order to show that the government in Warsaw did not concur with the decision of the Republic of Austria.

Why am I writing to you about this? Perhaps to underscore as strongly as I can that any kind of political persecution has, fundamentally, no influence on the course of cultural events. One cannot silence a writer or force compliance with the political powers against his will. You have been proving this for several years in your struggle for truth and the defence of freedom and human dignity. You are neither lonely nor alone, although it is clear that your situation is difficult and dangerous.

When I expressed my thanks in Vienna for the honour I was receiving, I was a free man. The course of events restored me to my normal life. But I understood clearly that this freedom was by no means enjoyed by all writers. I mentioned the names of two writers whose fate seemed to me particularly painful. I said, "It is the duty of our European self-respect to fight for the life of Salman Rushdie and for the freedom of Vaclav Havel."

I do not presume to compare my fate with yours, which is so difficult, or with that which Vaclav Havel had to endure for decades. As a writer I was interned for just a few months, and under less dramatic conditions, both in prison and in the internment camp. It is difficult to recall it at all when I think of Havel's prison experiences, and even more difficult next to the kind of threats that have been a part of your life for years now, like a nightmare. When I nevertheless write here of my own fate, then it is to show you that I understand very well what it means to be a writer who is suppressed and coerced, a citizen who is persecuted. I also know how painful it is to be the victim of a conspiracy and how much resistance the many years of continuous struggle require. Fortunately, the overwhelming majority of European and American writers are innocent of this knowledge, for fate has spared them personal experience of totalitarian power. In this sense I feel very close to you, and I feel a special solidarity with you, even though – I must admit this openly – I have not read your famous, excommunicated book. Fragments of your *The Satanic Verses* appeared in Polish translation only a few months ago. Maybe this sounds paradoxical, but I believe that just this fact (that I have not read your verses) makes my solidarity with you still more convincing, more evident, more unqualified.

What you wrote or did not write in *The Satanic Verses* is, after all, not very important, nor what you have expressed in your literary work or what you have remained silent about, what in these pages you have identified with or what you have rejected. You simply wrote what you wanted to write, that which you recognized as important from your point of view. In the pages of this book you published your understanding, your truth, your view of things; that is what writing is all about. In contrast to legal regulations, for example, writing is not binding. No one is obliged to read your books. If some people don't like you, absolutely nothing compels them to read what you have written. They can read something else, or nothing at all. They won't die of either. One can live a long time without having read a single book, a single newspaper or advertisement, or, yes, even a single prayer. It won't even give you a cold. The reading of your work, then, is entirely a matter of free choice for the reader. And, of course, one can be a complete fool if one wants, for literature is magnanimous. Neither you nor I intend to force someone to read our books. Perhaps they are not even worth reading. Who can be so sure today? In any case, there are people in the world who want to read all kinds of books, some better, some worse, and even some which others deem blasphemous. People have, then, the right to read what they want, just as you and I have the right to write what we want.

I am expressing truisms, making almost embarrassingly trite observations, and yet your fate proves that we even have to fight for that which seems obvious, for the most ordinary banalities. For that is what the most ordinary human freedom consists of, dear Mr Rushdie. The tragedy is that at the end of the twentieth century your situation raises a problem which our ancestors had already solved, or so a naïve dreamer from olden times might think. So then: they didn't solve it. I am thinking here of the basic human rights and freedoms, such as the right to express one's own opinion, the right to follow one's conscience, the right to chose one's own beliefs and the way of life that one is most attracted to and desires. Your situation proves that totalitarianiam is by no means dead. For decades I had to defend myself against totalitarianism of different stripes wanting to take my life, my freedom, my dignity, my profession, my parents' house. Or still worse: to convince me that there was no defence against totalitarianism, that one had to submit and sell your soul to the devil. Fortunately, I succeeded in defying their attempts, for life was merciful towards me. I was surrounded by decent and courageous people who gave me reliable support, and at my side was a loving and beloved wife, more resolute and courageous than I.

You, dear Mr Rushdie, have the support of a large portion of humanity, who understand ever more clearly that the attack on your rights is an attack on their own rights. Personally, I'm not overly fond of using the term "humanity", since those who talk too much about humanity tend to talk too little about humans. For that reason I do not want a discussion about your situation to become a discussion about the general situation of humanity. Rather it should be a discussion about your fate, above all. Nevertheless, I think that it is not enough to write you letters of solidarity. Personally, I am unfortunately not able to do anything more, for not only do I not have any heavy weapons, but last week I even lost my beloved penknife. As a writer, I am only able to raise my voice in order that the totalitarians from Tehran may finally give you your sacred peace. As you already know, I have experienced both brown and red totalitarianism, and now, thanks to your case, I am having problems with the green variety, to complete the circle. Green is a colour that in my country symbolizes hope. I hope, then, that the problem with Tehran is not only a matter of your fate or of mail which brings dozens of letters from writers, but that it becomes a political problem for all democratic governments and societies. This is a moral responsibility for all Europeans. After all, many evil things have been done with books. I was a boy when on the streets of German cities books were burned that were written by authors who did not please a certain club-foot by the name of Goebbels. A few years later, they were burning people in ovens. I was there. I saw it with my own eyes. And for just that reason I think that the self-respect of all Europeans rests on your case.

I greet you, Mr Rushdie, most sincerely.

Andrzej Szczypiorski

Gertrud Seehaus

Dear Salman Rushdie,

It is strange to look at the relatively informal salutation on this page, taut in my typewriter. After all, I don't know the person I am greeting in this manner. And yet, of course, I do know you, as indeed the entire world has come to know you. I have always looked and listened closely when, during the past three years, your words have penetrated into the world of streetcar conductors, movie and party-goers, birthday boys and girls, swimmers, strollers, pushers of baby carriages, visitors of churches, synagogues and mosques, people celebrating, or attending committee meetings – that world of which you haven't been a part for almost three years. It was extraordinary: news brought by an ultra-modern spaceship, a special isolation capsule cleverly manufactured by a combination of sinister, long-outdated ways of thinking and the most modern technology. All over the world one could see and hear a man who, as we well knew, had been excommunicated and made to be one of the loneliest people on earth.

Whenever I heard news of you, I asked myself: is he holding up? keeping hope? or giving in to despair? And I was always glad to find you active, engaged, creatively using the few opportunities available to you.

No writer who knows of your situation is unspared by it. It is as if old questions are asked again. What does freedom of opinion and expression mean when it is coupled with the question of pure, naked existence? How does a writer live with the virtual loss of his world, and how does that influence and change his writing?

Of course, no door to the world is opened for you when writers get together in the most varied places and discuss these questions. But perhaps it is a very small consolation to

103

know that you are in our thoughts in this way. And perhaps a bit of this world will make its way to you if we now send you our thoughts.

In the last decade I spent six years in Jerusalem, this unique meeting place of the three monotheistic religions, Judaism, Christianity, Islam. Although I gave up the Roman Catholic religion as an adult and no longer believe in the meaning of institutionalized religion, a place like Jerusalem almost forces one to think about religion and its effects. In the face of the wonderful philosophies of these three religions, and in the face of the ends in which these religions have been misused, I have written the following poem. I dedicate it to you, our dear colleague Salman Rushdie.

Don't Trust the Words
Innocence sucked out the words
Like marrow from bone
Husks stand about
Scaffolds of consonants
Gobs of stretched vowels
Stocking in the slime

God
a word for gunpowder
and the preparation of corpses
out of living bodies

God
they scream
swinging knives
setting fires
loading and shooting cannons
God
is their word

So as not to close this letter with the dark words of my poem, I want to express the hope that we will be able to celebrate your freedom in the not too distant future. When I get together in a few days with fellow writers, we will raise our glasses and drink to the freedom of thought and language. And to you, dear Salman Rushdie.

From one writer to another, your

Gertrud Seehaus

Dragan Velikic

Dear Salman Rushdie,

There is a Chinese fairy-tale whose themes are used by Marguerite Yourcenar in her story "How Wang-Fo Saved Himself". The main character, the painter Wang-Fo, lived as a vagabond in a huge empire, trading his pictures for food. But one day as he was sleeping, he was captured by soldiers and taken to the Emperor. On the throne sat a boy. He threatened to have the old man blinded, for the world that he depicted on his canvases was not the imperfect world in which people actually had to live. The young Emperor, however, had grown up in chambers in which his father displayed his large collection of the pictures of this very painter, Wang-Fo. Before he was to have Wang-Fo blinded for the lies that he spread through his art, the young Emperor ordered an unfinished canvas of the painter to be brought out. When Wang-Fo recognized the work of his youth, he also understood that it was only the sketch of a scene: a boat on the shore, grey cliffs, and a restless sea. Surrounded by guards, Wang-Fo began to paint. Suddenly he pushed the barely finished boat from the shore and sailed out to the sea that was as if of blue jade. And before the dumbfounded Emperor could order his courtiers to seize the painter, the boat became a tiny point, and Wang-Fo disappeared into the depths of his picture.

Is it not the dream of every artist ultimately to disappear into his work?

Three years have passed since the writer Salman Rushdie has been driven underground by a fanatic sentence. The ostensible reason for persecuting him is *The Satanic Verses*, a book that no reasonable person could find heretical. Nevertheless, the arrow of hatred has been shot, and its shadow leaves a mysterious trace on the face of the earth. In the meantime the voice of reason has lost intensity. We

107

have become dangerously used to the present situation, or even come to terms with it. But it must be clear to everyone that Rushdie was chosen as victim because he presents such a prominent target. Those who condemned him wanted to direct the attention to themselves. The "insults" of John Doe would never have been grounds for the anathema.

It is, nevertheless, a fact that although the anathema against Salman Rushdie continues to be in force, the voices of protest are becoming ever weaker. The cascades of anger against those who preach hatred are gradually drying up, and, with resignation, people are recognizing that the individual, after all, can do very little. And perhaps the individual really cannot do very much, but if he at least refuses to accept the present situation, he is already no longer helpless. The central question regarding the "Rushdie case" is how to help the condemned writer. How can we share the risk with him and thus parry the threat?

In the countryside in which I grew up, in Istria, there are small, windowless structures in the fields that serve the shepherds as shelter. These are *kazuni*, huts fashioned from ordinary boulders. The roofs are cone-shaped, made from small flagstones in such a way that the space is bridged without posts and arches but only by the imperceptible inching forward of each succeeding flagstone to the mid-point of the *kazun*.

This text, too, is meant as a small inching-forward in order to bridge over the abyss of hatred.

A completely different question: how much belief can there be in someone who condemns a writer to death? Is God a sack of sand whom any scoundrel can shove in front of him, like a breastplate? In any case, the threat that was pronounced over Salman Rushdie was intended to take from the writer his right to create the world from words, like a demiurge. But a writer is not God's competitor. He is only a part of the divine will to create, and sooner or later the scoundrels will stand alone out in the open, next to their breastplates, which they have provided with divine names.

While I am writing these lines, my countrymen are living

on hatred. But, as Spinoza says, hatred is only a sadness whose cause is mistakenly assumed to lie in the external world. This is the sadness of which Rushdie writes in his book *Haroun and the Sea of Stories*. This book is the true "answer" to hatred, for the arrow that has been shot is directed against all who, like the Chinese painter Wang-Fo, see the world differently. Fairy-tales are the common possession of us all, regardless of religion or skin colour. In this respect we sense that we all come from the same story. What separates us from the other creatures on the planet is our ability to speak. And it is precisely that which those who have sent the arrow of hate want to extinguish.

But how can it happen that the arrow will miss its goal?

By falling into the sea of stories, into just that sea of which Rushdie writes in his book. There, when the storyteller Rashid loses his gift, his son Haroun leads him to the invisible satellite, Kahani, there where the sea of stormy-streams is located, the largest library of the universe. They set out from a city that is so sad that its name has been forgotten. The sea of story-streams is a source at which every storyteller quenches his thirst. But on the invisible moon Kahani there are two zones: the world of Gup, lying completely in the sun, and the world of darkness, where the Chupwalas live. Theirs is the shadow-world, where books are kept under lock, and tongues are cut off. The Chupwalas have poisoned the story-rivers. At the end the powers of light are victorious after all, and the nameless city "remembers" its name. It is Kahani, which means: story. The only possible way, then, is to return to stories.

I am writing these lines in a country in which there are Gups and Chupwalas on each hostile side, separated by a zone of death in which arrows assert the name of God. And what can an artist do who sees in no soldier's uniform a garment suitable for himself? I believe that he can at least do something: he can go on telling his story and thus oppose the false messianic prophets of salvation. Furthermore, every work of art is only a reflection of the world that was created by God. This work, too, contains the boat that the arrow of hatred does not reach.

As solace I shall cite the sentence from Danilo Kis's novel, *The Hourglass*: "It is better to belong to the persecuted than to the persecutors."

Dragan Velikic

Joachim Walther

Dear Salman Rushdie,

Hans Magnus Enzensberger has said that even the Nazis had never called for someone's murder with a publicly advertized reward, as has been done for you. But they did, and they carried out the threat.

On 30 August 1933, the German philosopher and writer Theodor Lessing, living in exile in Czechoslovakia, was shot twice in the head, on which the Nazis had put a price of 80,000 Marks. A few days earlier he had written in the journal *Mein Kopf*: "My God! How many years have I had to hear about my head. In school they said I had a thick head. In the university it was a dunderhead. My colleagues tell me I'm pig-headed. A critic writes that it isn't a head for politics. Another, that it isn't a head for history. Still others say that my head lacks certain faculties. A faculty for metaphysics. For myth. For the cosmic. For mathematics. In short: everything about my head has been negative. I thought I was racking my brains, but I was just beating my head against the wall. And now 80,000 Marks! This reward my head will bring to others. I would have never thought it possible that so much money could be made with my head."

The gallows humour of the victim. The murderers, two religious fellow-travellers – a chauffeur and a forester – who were, by the way, in need of cash, but received instead only 50 Marks of the amount that was expected. They did get new names. They survived their employers, and the war. Later the forester lived in the Federal Republic of Germany, the chauffeur until his natural death in the GDR: here, too, German-German commonality, an indivisible history. Their employers, Hitler, Goebbels and Röhm, celebrated their victory at the Nürenberger Party Rally, and the applause of the screaming Germans fuelled the fire of the murderers. Even more macabre than this jubilation is what Thomas Mann, whom Lessing had once described as having a "gilt-edged soul", wrote in his diary: "I dread such an end, not because it is the end but because it is so wretched, and while it might be suitable for someone like Lessing, it would not be suitable for me."

But what had Lessing done that was so unforgivable? He fitted no category. He was no one's follower. And he irritated the political types with his philosophy of the deed, which he "cut into a hundred journals" in order to pay the rent. Lessing, the German Jew, who also wrote critically of the Jews and is therefore accused of Jewish anti-Semitism by those who are unable to read with nuance what has been written with nuance – of whom there are so many all over the world. Lessing, who called history and its grand illusionistic façades a myth, who early on called National Socialism a hollow vessel and Hitler – whom, moreover, he cast as Tarzan in a satire – a completely empty zero, which, though, like the eye of the hurricane, signifies the storm. But in a dictatorship satire is sacrilege. Lessing described President Hindenburg before his election as a nothing, behind which, so history teaches, a future Nero is always hidden. Lessing lifted one of the secrets of power – the aesthetisazation of politics, offering up a glut of symbols, flags, icons, phantasms and allegories to support all those forces that inhibit or numb reflection and intoxicate the blood with the flags of the people, the ringing bells of faith and orgies of romanticism. In a letter shortly before his death, he writes, "... the regime feels secretly that it has built upon a sandbank, and behind all their speeches, all their deeds of terror, stands a fear of the future".

Then, the final solutioners of the Third Reich, today the religious fanatics of God's state in Iran? Are they really both fashioned from equally extreme, one-dimensional ways of thinking, whose gruesome world-fantasy walks over corpses? Our glorious twentieth century already has the distinction of significantly enriching the panopticon of political criminals: Stalin, Hitler and Pol Pot, to name just a few madmen. They are all related, brothers in evil, in stature confusingly similar, but coloured differently: red, brown, and black.

Should the respected green of Islam enrich this Pandora's palette of outlaws?

I am writing to you from East Berlin. Our experience has made us East Germans sensitive, I hope, to the eternal simplifiers who want to reduce the complexity of life to their ideological-religious monorail. If their philosophy were only bleak, it would suffice to yawn; if it were powerless, laughter would be enough; but since it is fatal, and kills, it demands public resistance and solidarity among those who think differently.

Not coincidentally, I am presently writing a radio drama about Theodor Lessing. I have taken the liberty, dear Salman Rushdie, of dedicating it to you.

Yours in solidarity,

Joachim Walther

Lev Kopalev

Dear and esteemed Salman Rushdie,

Not only your colleagues – writers and journalists – owe you their thanks and admiration, but also the many people who are concerned about freedom of speech, about human dignity and human rights.

Your fate and your conduct are exemplary and represent the resistance of the free human spirit against power that is tyrannical and despises humanity.

Your situation is extraordinary: a totalitarian state, ruled by recklessly fanatical fundamentalists, openly threatens a writer with murder. But the significance of this threat extends far beyond your personal fate. It is a metaphor valid for all times and all places: wherever writers live, poetry is always both at home and alien, both celebrated and despised. The rulers may try to appropriate it with praise or to corrupt it by some other means, but poetry remains free and sovereign.

In our century far more writers have been persecuted than ever before, especially by Stalin's and Hitler's true believers or by their dully obedient thugs. In Russia and the other republics of the former Soviet Union in the years after 1918, almost 2,000 writers were hunted down, forced to emigrate, arrested and exiled. Many of them were even killed, among them the great writers Nikolay Gumilyov, Osip Mandelstam, Nikolay Klyuyav, Boris Pilnyak, Isaak Babel, Pavel Vasilev... In 1933 books were burned openly in Germany, over a thousand writers fled the country, others were arrested and some – Erich Mühsam, Theodor Lessing, Carl von Ossietzky – were murdered. Today, too, writers and journalists are threatened and persecuted in many countries. PEN International is working on behalf of over one hundred imprisoned writers.

Dear Salman Rushdie, your courageous resistance keeps

the memory of all martyrs of free speech alive. It is a declaration of allegiance to the freedom of the human spirit. I hope that the terrible danger that has been threatening you for these three years is soon banished. The memory of it shall remain a warning, a challenge for future generations.

Goethe said that a characteristic of the human spirit is that it "eternally moves the human spirit". You, too, move many children of the spirit. I am convinced that you will have students and successors and, always, new readers.

Sincerely,

Lev Kopalev

Tom Stoppard

On the third anniversary of the *fatwa*

The world of national sovereignties and of international law is not precisely the world of human rights. Nor does the world of human rights precisely contain the dimension of free expression. And yet, those worlds are intimately related when compared with the world of Islamic law as expounded and applied in present-day Iran.

It is bewildering that a member state of the United Nations can be openly and repeatedly, and with impunity, calling for the murder of a citizen of a foreign country.

It is bewildering – for we, too, have our laws, among them that incitement to murder is a criminal offence – that the cry should have been taken up in Britain, openly, repeatedly and with impunity. For to flout the law is to challenge Parliament.

We are not, I hope, a gathering of Western liberals come together to deplore attitudes uncongenial to Western liberalism. That particular circularity won't roll anywhere any more. The least ingratiating interpretation of this occasion would be that we are writers closing ranks for literature. Nor can I think of a quicker route to public indifference in this country.

Literature – the freedom of expression – is not unimportant to me but freedom of expression is not fundamental, as we acknowledge in our own laws. The proscription against writing which seeks to incite race hatred sits as comfortably in the Western liberal conscience as the proscription against falsely shouting "Fire!" in a crowded theatre. And of course to a theist free expression can never be fundamental: God never said, "Let there be freedom of thought and word."

What has happened here is a government invoking religious law, more specifically the word of God as revealed to Muhammad some thirteen-and-a-half centuries ago and written down in the book we know as the Koran, has sentenced a man to death for making (in the words of Archbishop of Canterbury) an outrageous slur on the Prophet.

Such extreme sanction is as strange and as repugnant to us as it was evidently reasonable to an Iranian diplomat who, three years ago, said: "Why do you find this behaviour strange?"

It's a question one is obliged to try to answer. To think it is not worth answering is to be ignorant of our own cultural history. The notion of tolerance as a human virtue, the concepts of liberty and pluralism as we venerate them today, were as unintelligible to St Augustine as to his contemporary Muhammad; and did not begin to find a place in our system of values for a thousand years after that.

"All these" – I'm quoting an essay by Isaiah Berlin – "all these are elements in a great mutation of Western thought and feeling that took place in the eighteenth century, the consequences of which appear in various counter-revolutions all too obvious in every sphere of life today."

Is that then our answer? That the eighteenth-century Enlightenment (and *we* chose to call it that: God didn't) made the discovery that man was perfectible, that change was progress, that progress was good; in short, that we Westerners have moved with the times and that Muslim fundamentalism has not?

Is that what we are saying? Evidently so. Our entire culture is saying it. I believe it. How do I substantiate to a sceptic that I am the one who has been enlightened? How can I be certain that one of the counter-revolutions mentioned by Isaiah Berlin will not overtake my children and leave *their* children in a very different culture but in a similar state of complacency, of certainty? You may counter: "And how many angels can dance on the nib of your pen? There is a man being hunted to death here." But I don't know how else to get at this. I think the punishment Salman Rushdie has suffered already, let alone the punishment which he has mercifully escaped for the last three years, far exceeds any offence which he has given, and for which he has apologized several times – it is deeply wrong on a level of humanness which binds us all, persecutors and persecuted. But I don't think it's wrong because of the supposed sanctity of the idea known as the freedom of expression; of literature.

Literature is not the only way to cause offence. If I were to open a pub and, through a combination of amazing ignorance and misplaced enthusiasm, were to call it "The Muhammad", I dare say a *fatwa* would be coming my way pretty smartly. Would the publican merit your intercession more than, or less than, the writer? I hope you would reply: equally.

I have never been comfortable with the idea that words have a preferential status over and above the discomfort they may give others simply because someone has chosen to write them. They may or may not have it; I don't see why they necessarily have it.

The issue here is not a man's right to publish: that is a particular local right which I would look to society to interpret in a tolerant, flexible and, yes, enlightened way. But the fundamental proposition is not that. It is that what has been done to Rushdie and what is threatened to him is intrinsically unjust.

The proper feeling is outrage. What is the proper action? What we have here, famously, is an opposition of two sets of mind without the common terms of value that enable even discourse, never mind resolution. On one side we hold up signs saying: "Irrational", "Fanatical", "Unenlightened"; while on the other side: "Why do you find this behaviour strange?"

The Koran is more than the doctrine of the faith; it is a handbook for the organization of the whole community in every detail. The Prophet was not the author of the words; he was merely the unique channel through which God chose to communicate, and with the death of the Prophet the source of the law dried up. Nothing could be added, subtracted or modified.

Scholarly interpretation offers the only tolerance. Hence the resistance to change which has brought us here. There is no place for an Islamic St Thomas Aquinas to incorporate the wisdom of classical antiquity. How then could there be a way to incorporate the very modern wisdom that freedom of expression is equally fundamental and universal?

Any argument from the fundamental right of free expression is a non-starter. This is to look at the problem from the wrong end. We should not be busy standing up for the rights we have accorded ourselves: we should be busy questioning the rights assumed by Iran, beginning with the assumption that Islamic law prevails over all other law in all other countries.

God did not choose to stop the world in the seventh century, and Iran with God's will has entered into a contract with the twentieth, with all its internationalism, its assemblies, its trade, its interdependence for peace and prosperity, its respect for sovereignty. Evidently that creates a problem for fundamentalism in Iran. But it is Iran's problem, and in the case of Salman Rushdie, Iran is trying to make it our problem.

These things need to be said by jurists and politicians. Evelyn Waugh, when he was once giving his views on capital punishment, was asked what he would think if he himself had to perform an execution. He replied that he would think it a most curiously arranged society in which the novelists were expected to execute the murderers.

I think it would be a curiously arranged society in which Salman Rushdie's fellow writers were expected to do the job which the world's statesmen exist to do.

Salman Rushdie

Reply

Before saying anything else I must thank, with all my heart, all the writers who wrote in my support, or in my defence, or in defence of the greater issues and principles raised by the so-called "Rushdie affair". (Oh, for the chance of ceasing to be an "affair" or a "case" and returning to the much harder task of being a writer plain and simple!) I must also thank *die tageszeitung* and the World Media project for their part in this initiative. I have often said that the existence of so many active and vocal defenders, and, beyond them, of millions of silent defenders is what has enabled me to deal with the difficulties of the past three years; and that is still absolutely true. So, thank you, Nadine Gordimer, for asking if we are returning to an age in which persecution is tolerated if it is backed by religion, and Kazuo Ishiguro, for concentrating (as so few people have concentrated, these past years) on *The Satanic Verses* I actually wrote, and Paul Theroux, for giving voice to your anger, and Johannes Simmel, for reminding us that the realities of big business are involved here, that human rights are all too easily steamrollered when fat contracts are up for grabs, and thank you, perhaps most of all, to Fahimeh Farsaie, for insisting that the attack against me and my work is only one battle in a larger war.

If there is more to say on a subject on which so much has already been said, it must be about this larger war. Fahimeh Farsaie criticized me, in her article, for failing to speak up for other writers, other artists who have been banned, jailed, tortured and even killed. The truth is that even

121

before Khomeini's *fatwa* I had been trying to say, as loudly as I could, that the Thought Police had become very powerful in the Muslim world today, and not only in the Muslim world; that the attempt to repress freedom of the imagination, freedom of thought, dissent, was growing in force. I have continued to say that just about every time I have had a chance to say anything, and will go on doing so.

The point regarding the case of *The Satanic Verses* is this: because of the attention paid to it, it has become the symbol and the archetype of all the other cases of repression. Those mediaeval dogs of war, "blasphemy" and "heresy", have been let slip – and we must not forget that throughout human history "blasphemy" and "heresy" have been used to shackle and muzzle the human spirit, the free voice. The reason why this battle must be won, why the *fatwa* and its attendant menaces must go, is that the victory would be at once actual (which would be very nice for me) and representative – it would strike a powerful blow in that larger war. And if the battle were lost, it would be a bad moment in the larger conflict. We must win because we cannot lose; what is at stake is nothing less than our minds.

"The peculiar evil of silencing the expression of an opinion," wrote John Stuart Mill in his classic essay, "On Liberty", "is that it is robbing the human race, posterity as well as the existing generation – those who dissent from the opinion, still more than those who hold it. [For] if the opinion be right, they are deprived of the opportunity of exchanging error for truth; if wrong, they lose what is almost as great a benefit, the clearer perception and livelier impression of truth produced by its collision with error."

The particular case of imaginative writing requires the addition of a few extra words to Mill's great text. For in imaginative writing, the normal situation is that no one opinion is consistently advocated. In this respect the creative process is not unlike the processes of free societies, which are by their nature divided, plural, even quarrelsome; they are societies in motion, and with motion comes tension, friction. Free peoples strike sparks, and those sparks are the best evidence of freedom's presence. Totalitarianism always seeks to halt the motion of society, to snuff out its spark, to replace the many truths of liberty by the one truth of power.

In the creative process, many attitudes, many world-views jostle and conflict within the writer, and from these frictions the spark, the work of art, is born. This inner multiplicity, this crowd within, is often very difficult for artists to bear, let alone explain. We remember Diderot's struggle between atheistic rationalism and his own spiritual needs. "It infuriates me," he wrote, "to be enmeshed in a devilish philosophy which my mind is forced to accept but my heart to disown." Dostoevsky also agonized about the coexistence within him of absolute faith and absolute unbelief. And William Blake, noticing that in *Paradise Lost* John Milton was better at describing Hell than Heaven, said approvingly that Milton, that devout genius, was as a poet naturally of the devil's party. Within every artist – perhaps within every human imagination – there exists, to paraphrase Blake, a marriage between Heaven and Hell.

The case of *The Satanic Verses*, as many of the writers who contributed to the campaign noticed, contains, at its heart, an appalling *shapeliness*. Here is a novel about the conflicts and tensions between – and also within – the secular and religious views of the world, which has become engulfed in precisely those conflicts. As Kurt Vonnegut might say: so it goes.

And behind *The Satanic Verses*, behind all the letters my fellow-writers wrote, stands our knowledge that the attempt to create shape out of the thick soup of human experience, the constant re-shaping of meaning that the artistic process insists upon, cannot be surrendered to any gang of policemen, no matter how big their guns. This is – "fundamentally", if I may use so fundamentalist a word – a battle of wills. The most inspiring and strengthening thing about the many open letters is that they show precisely the kind of will that is required to hold out against tyranny and vilification and murder: the will to win.

Fiction, Fact and the *Fatwa*

Foreword

In September 1988 *India Today* and *Sunday* published interviews with Indian-born, British author, Salman Rushdie, about his forthcoming novel, *The Satanic Verses*, due to be published in the United Kingdom on 26 September.

Muslim opposition MPs, Khurshi Alam Khan and Syed Shahabuddin, began a vigorous campaign to ban the book, holding rallies and demonstrations. Aslam Ejaz, of the Islamic Foundation in Madras, wrote to Faiyazuddin Ahmad in Leicester, England, suggesting that a similar campaign be launched in Britain.

On 5 October 1988 the Indian Finance Ministry announced the banning of *The Satanic Verses* under Section 11 of the Indian Customs Act, adding that the ban did not detract from the literary and artistic merit of Rushdie's work.

Virtually every leading Indian newspaper and magazine deplored the ban; *The Hindu*'s editorial called it "a philistine decision", and a leader in the *Indian Express* called it "thought control".

In an open letter to Prime Minister Rajiv Gandhi (published in the *Indian Express* 13 October) Salman Rushdie expressed his concern that the government of India had banned his book and accused its detractors of extremism and political manipulation. The *Economic and Political Weekly* of 22 October stated that the ban was a political decision and accused Prime Minister Gandhi of capitulating because of the impending November elections. Writers, editors and publishers protested the ban in a letter to the Prime Minister, calling it ill-conceived and hastily executed.

In South Africa, Salman Rushdie was due to attend the *Weekly Mail* Book Week in Johannesburg and Cape Town, an invitation extended by the *Weekly Mail* and the Congress of South African writers (COSAW). When the invitation became public knowledge, Muslim groups protested strong-

127

ly to the organizers of the Book Week and thinly-veiled threats of violence were made; others sought to mediate between Salman Rushdie's hosts and the extremists. On 28 October 1988 a notice in the government *Gazette* announced the banning of the book under section 47(2)b of the Publications Act – the section dealing with blasphemy. Under pressure from a wide range of Muslim organizations, and after a series of meetings, COSAW decided to withdraw its invitation to the author, unable to guarantee his safety. Despite the pressure and several bomb threats, the *Weekly Mail* did not withdraw its invitation, holding that Salman Rushdie had been invited long before the publication of *The Satanic Verses* and that "he was chosen because of his standing as a writer and because of his active concern over the issue of censorship". The theme of Rushdie's proposed opening address at the *Weekly Mail* Book Week was to have been "Wherever they burn books, they will also burn people." However, Salman Rushdie participated in the event, via a telephone link. The panel discussion of which he was thus part was attended by an audience of 300 people.

In the UK, objectionable passages from *The Satanic Verses* were brought to the attention of Muslim organizations, mosques, and Muslim ambassadors, who lobbied Viking/Penguin for the immediate withdrawal of the book. On 11 October 1988 the UK Action Committee on Islamic Affairs was founded to mobilize public opinion against the novel. In November the 46-nation Organization of the Islamic Conference General Secretariat urged member states to take strong action against the book's publisher and author if they failed to withdraw the work.

During November, the governments of Bangladesh and Sudan banned *The Satanic Verses*, which won the Whitbread "best novel" award on 8 November.

In December a protest rally, organized by the Islamic Defence Council, was held in London and similar rallies followed in British towns and cities which had sizeable Muslim populations. On 14 December, the government of Sri Lanka banned the novel. On 14 January 1989 Muslims in

Bradford, Yorkshire, burned a copy of *The Satanic Verses*, in order to draw attention to their grievances. This act caused a storm of protest, the media immediately responded and the controversy became world-wide news.

On 8 February Pakistan's National Assembly banned the novel. The ban was followed by a series of violent protests against Salman Rushdie and his novel in Bombay and Dacca. On 13 February one person was killed and over 100 were injured during a riot in Kashmir. On 12 February some 2,000 protesters tried to storm the US Embassy in Islamabad, in protest at the forthcoming publication of the book in the US. In response to attacks by stones and bricks, police opened fire, killing at least five people and injuring more than 100. This confrontation was televised world-wide, including in Tehran.

Carmel Bedford
Editor Article 19
Secretary ICDSR

Fiction, fact and the *fatwa*

14 February 1989: Day 1
Ayatollah Ruhollah Khomeini of Iran pronounces a *fatwa* (religious edict) on Salman Rushdie and his publishers which is broadcast on Tehran radio: "I inform the proud Muslim people of the world that the author of *The Satanic Verses* book which is against Islam, the Prophet and the Koran, and all involved in its publication who were aware of its content, are sentenced to death." Anyone who dies in the cause of ridding the world of Rushdie, he says, "will be regarded as a martyr and go directly to heaven".

Salman Rushdie and his wife, author Marianne Wiggins, go into hiding and are placed under armed guard.

15 February 1989: Day 2
Iran proclaims a national day of mourning in protest against *The Satanic Verses*. Thousands of demonstrators chanting "death to Britain" stone the British Embassy in Tehran. Iranian Foreign Minister Ali Akbar Velayati calls calls upon all Muslim countries to close British and American cultural centres. All Viking/Penguin books are banned from Iran.

Hojatoleslam Hassani Sanei, an Iranian cleric of the 15 Khordad Foundation, offers a US$3 million reward to any Iranian and $1 million to any foreigner who kills Salman Rushdie.

Viking/Penguin's New York offices are evacuated for an hour after an anonymous bomb threat. Salman Rushdie cancels a planned three-week US tour to promote *The Satanic Verses*.

Harold Pinter leads a delegation of writers to 10 Downing Street to protest the *fatwa* against Salman Rushdie.

PEN American Center condemns "the extreme action the Ayatollah Khomeini has taken in calling for the death of a writer for exercising his internationally recognized right to freedom of artistic expression".

16 February 1989: Day 3
A European Economic Council resolution notes "with horror the appeal of Ayatollah Khomeini to Muslims to kill the author Salman Rushdie and the publishers of his book, *The Satanic Verses*" and demands that the Council "make plain to the Iranian government that if attempts are made on the lives of Mr Rushdie and his publishers, severe sanctions will be taken against Iranian interests and that force will be used to bring the criminals concerned to justice".

The UK government protests "in the strongest terms" to the Iranian Chargé d'Affaires in London over Ayatollah Khomeini's statement which is "totally unacceptable". Sir Geoffrey Howe, the Foreign Secretary, says that ties with Tehran will be impossible if it "failed to respect international standards of behaviour".

The UK Arts Council issues a statement calling for tolerance and understanding, and accepting that the Islamic community have the freedom to criticize Mr Rushdie's book, the statement adds: "It is, however, intolerable that there should be threats of physical violence against Mr Rushdie."

Pakistan lodges protests against *The Satanic Verses* with both the UK and the United States and demands that the novel should be banned.

The French Human Rights League condemns the *fatwa* against Salman Rushdie and his publishers and appeals to French politicians to denounce it.

17 February 1989: Day 4
Iranian President Ali Khamenei suggests that if Salman Rushdie repents and apologizes to Muslims: "it is possible that the people may pardon him".

In London, Iran's Chargé d'Affaires describes Ayatollah Khomeini's execution order as "purely a religious statement", not meant as a political gesture against Britain.

The West German government announces the recall of its

Chargé d'Affaires in Tehran. The Iranian ambassador in Bonn is summoned to the Foreign Ministry and told that West Germany severely condemns the *fatwa*.

In the US, bookstores B. Dalton, Waldenbook, and Noble decide not to sell *The Satanic Verses*. After telephone threats, Viking/Penguin closes its US offices to install a new security system.

18 February 1989: Day 5
Salman Rushdie issues a statement: "As author of *The Satanic Verses* I recognize that Muslims in many parts of the world are genuinely distressed by the publication of my novel. I profoundly regret the distress that publication has occasioned to sincere followers of Islam. Living as we do in a world of many faiths this experience has served to remind us that we must all be conscious of the sensibilities of others."

Mr Sayed Abdul Quddis, joint secretary of the Bradford Council of Mosques, says: "This is good news and we are glad and satisfied. We want to keep in harmony and peace. But Rushdie should have apologized in the first instance weeks ago. If he had been polite, it would not have erupted." Dr Hesham El-Essawy, Chairman of the Islamic Society for the Promotion of Religious Tolerance, says: "I regard it as an apology and it should pave the way out of this crisis. I now hope that it will resolve the problems between Iran and Britain." The Bradford Council of Mosques describes the author's statement as "not a sincere apology but a further insult to the Muslim community as a whole". Dr Kalim Siddiqui, Director of the Muslim Institute in London, upholds the *fatwa*.

France recalls its Chargé d'Affaires from Tehran.

19 February 1989: Day 6
In a statement from Iran, Ayatollah Khomeini says that Salman Rushdie's statement falls short of the public repentance required for a pardon and adds: "It is incumbent on every Muslim to employ everything he has got, his life and his wealth, to send him to hell."

Some 100 intellectuals from Arabic and Islamic cultures demonstrate against the *fatwa* pronounced on Salman Rushdie, in the Human Rights Square, Paris.

20 February 1989: Day 7
The Foreign Ministers of the 12 EC countries issue a joint declaration on Iranian threats against Mr Rushdie and his publishers: "The Foreign Ministers view these threats with the gravest concern. They condemn this incitement to murder as an unacceptable violation of the most elementary principles and obligations that govern relations among sovereign States. They underline that such behaviour is contrary to the Charter of the United Nations. They believe that fundamental principles are at stake. They reaffirm that the Twelve have the fullest respect for the religious feelings of all peoples. They remain fully committed to the principles of freedom of thought and expression within their territories. They will ensure protection of the life and properties of their citizens. In no case will they accept attempts to violate these basic rights. The Twelve express their continuing interest in developing normal constructive relations with the Islamic Republic of Iran, but if Iran shares this desire, it has to declare its respect for international obligations and renounce the use or the threatened use of violence. Meanwhile the Foreign Ministers of the Twelve decided to simultaneously recall their Heads of Mission in Tehran for consultations and to suspend exchanges of high-level visits. The Iranian Authorities will be informed of the above in the hope that the universal values of tolerance, freedom and respect for international law will prevail. The Twelve look to the Iranian authorities to protect the life and safety of all community citizens in their country."

United Nations Secretary General Javier Perez de Cuellar appeals for the death threat to be lifted.

UNESCO's Director-General, Federico Mayor, declares: "For UNESCO, as a world-wide forum for dialogue and understanding, freedom of creation, of opinion and of expression, with respect for convictions, beliefs and religions, is essential. A house of freedom, UNESCO is troubled whenever the fundamental right of the individual to express his or her thoughts is threatened. A house of creativity, it has a sense of loss whenever the human imagination is condemned to silence. A house of peace, it suffers whenever violence is unleashed. It is every person's duty to respect other people's religions; it is also every person's duty to respect other people's freedom of expression. Whatever the offence may be, no incitement to violence, from whatever source, is admissible. The human community thrives on its differences, be they of race, language, belief or culture. Such differences are our common wealth; respect for them by one and all is the guarantee of our survival."

The International Committee for the Defence of Salman Rushdie and his Publishers (ICDSR) is founded at a meeting in London attended by organizations and individuals representing writers, publishers, booksellers, journalists, trade unions and human rights groups whose first initiative is the denunciation of the *fatwa* as "armed censorship".

20 February 1989: Day 8
Iran recalls its envoys from the 12 EC countries in retaliation for the EC's decision to withdraw its heads of mission from Tehran. The Norwegian Ambassador in Iran is recalled for consultations.

At a press conference, US President George Bush, referring to *The Satanic Verses* says: "However offensive that book may be, inciting murder and offering rewards for its perpetration are deeply offensive to the norm of civilized behaviour..."

22 February 1989: Day 9
Ayatollah Khomeini declares on Iranian radio: "an economic blockade by the EC won't stop Iran from its intention to execute the divine order".

The Hague, Netherlands: 850 intellectuals sign a petition asking the Dutch government to respond against the condemnation of *The Satanic Verses*.

Die tageszeitung publishes the first extracts of *The Satanic Verses* on its front page. German authors send a telegram to

Chancellor Helmut Kohl: "We request that the German government pressurize the government of Iran to rescind the death threat through economic measures if necessary."

The Association of American Publishers, the American Booksellers Association and the American Library Association take a full-page advertisement in the *New York Times* which states: "Today is the publication date of Salman Rushdie's book *The Satanic Verses*. Free People Write Books, Free People Publish Books, Free People Sell Books, Free People Buy Books, Free People Read Books. In the spirit of America's commitment to free expression we inform the public that this book will be available to readers at bookshops and libraries throughout the country."

PEN American Center presents public readings from *The Satanic Verses* in New York. Readers include Susan Sontag, Aryeh Neier, Claire Bloom, Norman Mailer and Larry McMurtry. PEN Center USA West holds a public reading from *The Satanic Verses* in the lobby of the *Los Angeles Times*. Readers include Betty Friedan, Ray Bradbury, Alvin Toffler, Lawrence Thornton, T. Coraghessan Boyle and Roberta Smoodin.

A joint statement by the Irish Writers' Union and the Irish Translators' Association: "views with abhorrence the recent 'death penalty' passed on Salman Rushdie" and appeals to all Irish writers and publishers to express solidarity with the author.

23 February 1989: Day 10
Canada recalls its Chargé d'Affaires from Tehran.

French President Mitterand denounces Ayatollah Khomeini's fanaticism. *Liberation* publishes a petition from 155 writers expressing their solidarity with Salman Rushdie. *Liberation*, *Le Nouvel Observateur* and *Le Monde* publish chapters I, II, and IV of *The Satanic Verses*.

More than 80 prominent Asians in Britain, including artists, writers and academics, some of them Muslim, sign a statement defending the right of Salman Rushdie to publish *The Satanic Verses*. Their statement deplores the recent public book burnings and attempts to suppress its distribution and adds: "Such agitation, directed at suppressing dissent, can offer succour only to those who wish to undo Britain's development towards a truly multi-cultural society."

24 February 1989: Day 11

Following anti-Rushdie demonstrations in Bombay, 12 Muslim rioters are shot dead by police and about 50 are injured.

Sir Sridath Ramphal, Secretary-General of the Commonwealth Secretariat, writes to the ICDSR: "Nothing is more important at the moment in the issue over Salman Rushdie's *The Satanic Verses* than that those in authority in Iran should be left in no doubt that directing and rewarding the killing of Rushdie is wholly unacceptable to the rest of the world. There is no country in the Commonwealth that supports or acquiesces in such conduct. Even countries that have banned the book's publication draw the line at incitement to its author's assassination. Iran must not believe that this is a quarrel only with Britain. All people, all countries, that value the norms of free societies and look for a world governed by law, are outraged by Tehran's incitement to murder and join in demanding its withdrawal."

British Muslims march in Manchester in protest at *The Satanic Verses*.

Wole Soyinka, the 1986 Nobel Prize winner for literature, in a statement to Nigerian newspapers, says civilized nations have a duty to expel Iranian diplomats from their territories because of the death threat against Salman Rushdie. "If Rushdie is unnaturally and prematurely silenced, the creative world will launch its own Jihad. It has the will and the resources and imagination."

In South Africa, the Muslim Youth Movement and the Call for Islam group express "unequivocal condemnation" of *The Satanic Verses* but distance themselves from Ayatollah Khomeini's *fatwa*. More than 330 people, including prominent South African writers, publishers and journalists, sign a statement in support of Salman Rushdie.

25 February 1989: Day 12
Iran cancels a British trade exhibition, planned for Tehran in March, over the Rushdie affair. In Bucharest, writer Neagu Udroiu, secretary of the press agency Agerpress, calls on Iranian President Ali Khamenei to renounce the *fatwa*.

26 February 1989: Day 13
An anonymous caller from "the Muslim Revolutionary Forces" tells Agence France Presse (AFP) in Beirut to announce that "all the revolutionary forces in the world have decided to uphold the *fatwa* and have asked a group of people to execute the sentence". The Iranian news agency IRNA's correspondent in Madrid declares: "the day of [Rushdie's] execution is already fixed".

In Moscow, writers demonstrate against the *fatwa* outside the Iranian Embassy.

More than 1,000 Muslims in Paris demonstrate against *The Satanic Verses* and call for Salman Rushdie's death. Thousands of US Muslims protest in New York against *The Satanic Verses*.

27 February 1989: Day 14
Tara Arts Group, a UK Asian national touring theatre company, deplores the burning of *The Satanic Verses* in Bradford and the attempts underway to suppress its distribution, and repudiates the death sentence on the author and his publishers.

Following the Paris demonstration against Salman Rushdie, French Prime Minister M. Rocard announces that any new provocation to violence and murder will be punished. Following a mass demonstration by Muslims in Oslo, threats are issued to publisher William Nygaard and the Norwegian translator of *The Satanic Verses*.

28 February 1989: Day 15
In Pakistan, the weekly *Takbeer* is banned for having published extracts from *The Satanic Verses*. A Pakistani security guard is killed in a bomb attack on the British Council Library in Karachi. In Srinagar, India, a demonstration

137

against police repression of the 24 February demonstration in Bombay leaves one person dead and 7 people injured. Syria bans *The Satanic Verses*. The USSR proposes to mediate between Iran and Western countries on the *fatwa*.

A firebomb and an incendiary device are thrown through the windows of Cody's Books and Waldenbooks in Berkeley, California. The offices of the *Riverdale Press* in the Bronx, New York, which had published an editorial criticizing book chains for withdrawing *The Satanic Verses* from sale, are severely damaged by a firebomb.

US Senators Moynihan, Mitchell, Dole, Pell, Helms, Sanford, Gorton, Graham, Simon and D'Amato submit resolution 72 in the Senate, condemning the threats against the author and publishers of *The Satanic Verses* and expressing the Senate's commitment to "protect the right of any person to write, publish, sell, buy and read books without fear of intimidation or violence". It is passed unanimously.

The Iranian Majlis (parliament) votes almost unanimously to sever all diplomatic relations with Britain.

1 March 1989: Day 16
The Moroccan authorities seize the March issue of the French-language *Kalima* magazine, published in Casablanca, which includes Moroccan writers' statements supporting Salman Rushdie. Pakistan bans Salman Rushdie from visiting the country. Lebanon, Kenya and Brunei ban *The Satanic Verses*.

UK Education Secretary, Kenneth Baker, at a meeting in Bradford, appeals for racial and religious tolerance in the wake of the Rushdie affair, and adds: "Those who wish to make their home in Britain, to contribute to our society and to prosper within it, cannot deny to others the very freedoms which drew them to this country in the first place."

Some 1,500 Norwegian writers, authors, journalists, editors, publishers, translators and critics sign the international appeal protesting the death threat to Salman Rushdie.

The Latvian SSR Union of Writers writes to the President of Iran expressing concern about the future of world literature and human relations in the light of the conflict ensuing after the publication of *The Satanic Verses*:

2 March 1989: Day 17
The ICDSR publishes a *World Statement* in defence of Salman Rushdie and his publishers, signed by 1,000 internationally-known writers, calling for the right to freedom of expression as embodied in Article 19 of the Universal Declaration of Human Rights. Whilst appreciating the distress the book has aroused and deeply regretting the loss of life associated with the ensuing conflict, the *Statement* calls upon world opinion to support the right of all people to express their ideas and beliefs and to discuss them with their critics on the basis of mutual tolerance, free from censorship, intimidation and violence. Furthermore, it requests all world leaders to continue to repudiate the threats made against Salman Rushdie and his publishers and to take firm action to ensure that these threats are withdrawn. The *World Statement* is published, free of charge, in 62 newspapers and magazines throughout the world.

The Australian Free Speech Committee organizes a picket outside Symocks and Angus and Robertson bookshops in Sydney to protest their refusal to sell *The Satanic Verses*.

3 March 1989: Day 18
In Dhaka, Bangladesh, thousands of Muslims hold a rally to protest against *The Satanic Verses*. Some 100 are reported injured when police open fire. In Kashmir, India, confrontations between police and Muslim demonstrators leave one person dead and 84 injured. Pakistan bans *Time* and *Newsweek* "for publishing reviews of the proscribed book... along with blasphemous quotations therefrom". In Istanbul, Turkey, a large rally protests against *The Satanic Verses*.

4 March 1989: Day 19
Salman Rushdie is made an honorary member of the Yugoslav Writers' Association. French actress Isabelle Adjani reads an extract of *The Satanic Verses* at the "Césars ceremony" when she is awarded the prize for "best actress".

Muslims demonstrate against Salman Rushdie and *The*

Satanic Verses in Bonn, Bangkok, Karachi, Srinagar, Rotterdam and Stockholm.

5 March 1989: Day 20
Muslims march through Keighley, West Yorkshire, and burn placards in a rally calling for *The Satanic Verses* to be banned. Palestinian guerilla leader, Ahmed Jibril, declares: "We in the PFLP-GC will confront this new conspiracy and work to execute the legal action against Rushdie." Muslim organizations in Sydney, Australia, hold protests calling for the book to be banned.

The Vatican expresses its solidarity with people who have been injured in their faith.

6 March 1989: Day 21
Colonel Muammar al-Qaddafi of Libya endorses the *fatwa*.

7 March 1989: Day 22
Iran breaks off diplomatic relations with Britain. Thailand bans *The Satanic Verses*.

8 March 1989: Day 23
Susan Sontag, on behalf of PEN American Center, gives testimony before the Subcommittee on International Terrorism, Senate Foreign Relations Committee, on the subject of writers' responses to the controversy over Salman Rushdie's *The Satanic Verses*, their views of the government's response, and their concerns that the events of recent weeks may affect freedom of expression in the US from now on.

US Ambassador Nicholas A. Veliotes, President of the Association of American Publishers, testifies before the Senate Foreign Relations Committee, reaffirming that "Any real concession to terrorists begets more terrorism."

Moscow News publishes a petition appealing to Ayatollah Khomeini to show "clemency" towards Salman Rushdie. The petition is signed by more than a dozen Soviet intellectuals, including Andrei Sakharov and Roald Sagdeiev, an adviser to President Gorbachev.

9 March 1989: Day 24
The [West] Berlin Academy of Arts refuses to allow the use
of its rooms for a Salman Rushdie Solidarity event because
of reservations concerning security. Günter Grass and
philosopher Günter Anders resign from the academy, which
is said to have "renounced its obligations to the past".

10 March 1989: Day 25
German authors hold a reading of extracts from *The Satanic
Verses* under the patronage of the German PEN Center. Five
hundred Iranians, living in Berlin, hold a Solidarity With
Rushdie event at the Technical University.

13 March 1989: Day 28
The Chief Metropolitan Magistrate in London refuses to
grant Abdul Hussain Choudhury summonses against
Salman Rushdie and his publishers, Viking/Penguin, alleg-
ing "blasphemous libel and seditious libel at the common
law", and rules that the law of blasphemy in England and
Wales protects only the Christian religion.
   Tanzania and Indonesia ban *The Satanic Verses.*

14 March 1989: Day 29
A 36-hour "Stand Against Censorship" vigil begins at the
United Nations in New York, organized by the National
Writers Union, Article 19, the Authors Guild and PEN
American Centre. Participants include Ariel Dorfman,
Edward Asner, William Styron, Kurt Vonnegut, Philip
Caputo, Alix Kates Shulman and Nat Hentoff.
   Fifth Avenue in New York is sealed off after a bomb
threat to a large bookshop.
   Singapore bans *The Satanic Verses.*

15 March 1989: Day 30
As part of a worldwide day of action for Salman Rushdie, a
group of writers present a book containing the ICDSR
World Statement and a petition calling for support for the
author to the Secretary General of the United Nations.
Writers including Kazuo Ishiguro, Russell Hoban, Michael

Holroyd, Francis King, Martin Marix Evans, Harold Pinter, Bernice Rubens, Graham Swift, Marina Warner, Fay Weldon, Arnold Wesker, Hanif Kureishi, Iraj Jannatie Ataie, Shotuh Mirzadeji, Esmail Noori Ala, Moris Farhi and Ben Okri take part in a vigil outside the UN office.

16 March 1989: Day 31
UK Prime Minister Margaret Thatcher's office replies to Lady Antonia Fraser of the ICDSR: "Before Britain's relationship with Iran can be repaired, Iran must show clearly that it is willing to meet its international obligations and to renounce the use or threat of violence against the citizens and interests of other countries."

The International Book Fair of radical black and Third World books opens at Bradford Community Arts Centre. In his opening address, John La Rose, poet, writer and founder of the black publishing company New Beacon Books, reads a telex he sent to Prime Minister Thatcher on behalf of his company the day following the issue of the *fatwa*. The telex concluded: "We utterly condemn the fascist practice of book burning and we request that the British government give full protection to Salman Rushdie."

In Riyadh, Saudi Arabia, the Islamic Conference Organization bans Viking/Penguin publications in 45 Muslim countries in protest at the publisher's refusal to withdraw *The Satanic Verses*, but refuses to support Iran over the death threat to Salman Rushdie and his publishers.

17 March 1989: Day 32
Sudanese Muslims demonstrate in Khartoum against *The Satanic Verses*.

21 March 1989: Day 36
In Australia, Sutherland Shire Council libraries withdraw *The Satanic Verses* following a series of bomb threats.

EC decision to allow member countries to send ambassadors back to Iran. Spanish Foreign Minister Francisco Fernandez Ordoñez, President of the EC Council, says : "In any contacts with Iranian authorities, the ambassadors will express the solidarity of the community, which stands by its 20 February declaration."

29 March 1989: Day 44
The spiritual leader of Belgium's Muslims, Abdullah Ahdal, a Saudi Arabian, and his deputy, Salim Bahri, a Tunisian, are shot and killed. Mr Ahdal had received threats after he was reported as saying on Belgian TV that the death sentence pronounced by Ayatollah Khomeini against Mr Rushdie was aimed at public opinion within Iran but that in Europe there was freedom of expression.

9 April 1989: Day 55
In London, Collet's Penguin Bookshop and Dillons Bookshop are firebombed.

12 April 1989: Day 58
Publication of the Norwegian translation of *The Satanic Verses*, six weeks prior to plan, is met by angry reactions among the Muslim community. Publisher William Nygaard's home, his publishing house and staff are placed under constant surveillance by the police. Two Norwegian bookstores are set on fire and a third receives a bomb threat.

18 April 1989: Day 64
At a public debate held in Titograd, Yugoslavia, Idriz Demirovic, President of the Supreme Council of the Yugoslav Islamic Community, comments that although Salman Rushdie has published untruths about Muhammed and offended Muslims in *The Satanic Verses*, no one can sentence him as it is the sole right of the Shari'a court.

24 April 1989: Day 70
In Paris, the Arab Association of Human Rights issues a statement appealing for wisdom in the Rushdie affair: "No blasphemy does as much damage to Islam and to Muslims as the call for the murder of a writer. Disturbed by the latest developments in this affair and the ways they are being interpreted, we call on all those who, like us, are attached to

Arab-Muslim civilization, to reject without qualification calls for murder which designate all Muslims as potential assassins; confront the hysteria in the media and elsewhere which is provoking racial confusion and prejudice against Arab and Muslim cultures and peoples; and reverse the escalation (of this situation) which is endangering understanding between peoples, and endangering the situation of immigrant communities in France and Europe." The statement is signed by many writers, including Naguib Mahfouz, journalists, film-makers, poets, actors and academics.

25 April 1989: Day 71
In Norway, 25 Muslim organizations take legal action against publisher H. Aschehoug & Co.

26 April 1989: Day 72
Iqbal Sacranie, Convenor of the UK Action Committee on Islamic Affairs, states in London that "paperback publication [of *The Satanic Verses*] would aggravate an already serious situation. It would be a highly insensitive act at a time of increasing tension."

30 April 1989: Day 76
After describing Ayatollah Khomeini as a terrorist, Nobel Prize-winning author Naguib Mahfouz receives death threats from Sheikh Omar Abdel Rahman, leader of the Islamic Jihad group which assassinated President Anwar Sadat in September 1981.

6 May 1989: Day 82
Launch in Britain of Women Against Fundamentalism, a network which aims to challenge the rise of fundamentalism in all religions. Women's groups involved in the campaign include: Southall Black Sisters, Brent Asian Women's Refuge and Iranian women's organizations in Britain. They oppose suppression of *The Satanic Verses*.

The Booksellers Association of Great Britain and Ireland passes a resolution at its annual general meeting: "This conference approves with admiration the courage and persis-

tence of the publishers of *The Satanic Verses* in ensuring that
this book continues to be available to the public, despite
threats to the lives of those responsible for it, and fully supports members of the Booksellers Association who continue
to stock and sell it while and where demand justifies it. The
Conference condemns unequivocally any attempts to suppress books published within the law, especially if such
attempts involve violence or the threat of violence."

21 May 1989: Day 97
Abbey's bookshop in Sydney, Australia, is firebombed; man-
ager Peter Milne had received death threats after he was
quoted in the media as saying that he would continue to sell
The Satanic Verses after Dymocks and Angus and Robertsons
had decided to withdraw their copies from sale.

26 May 1989: Day 102
"Voices for Salman Rushdie" is launched at a press conference in the House of Commons. The group is campaigning
"For the right to dissent against racism and fundamentalism" and is backed by a wide variety of groups and individuals including those from black and ethnic minorities,
Iranian dissidents, London Irish Women's Centre, Southall
Black Sisters, Women Against Fundamentalism, socialists,
feminists, civil libertarians and writers.

27 May 1989: Day 103
Led by the British Muslim Action Front, 30,000 Muslims
demonstrate in Hyde Park, London, and, carrying placards,
portraits of Ayatollah Khomeini and effigies of Salman
Rushdie, march to Parliament Square to petition for an
extension of the blasphemy law to include Islam. Barbara
Smoker of the National Secular Society and Nicolas Walter
of the Rationalist Press Association hold banners calling for
Free Speech and are attacked by Muslim demonstrators.
Pickets from Women Against Fundamentalism are also
attacked and police have to move in to defend them. A
dozen police are injured and there are over 100 arrests.

30 May 1989: Day 106
Dr Kalim Siddiqui upholds the *fatwa* against Salman
Rushdie on a television programme, adding: "We hit back.
We sometimes hit back first."

The International Federation of Journalists adopts a resolution which condemns the appeal to kill Salman Rushdie.

4 June 1989: Day 111
Dr Kalim Siddiqui declares that the death sentence passed
on Salman Rushdie will remain, despite the death on the
previous day of Ayatollah Khomeini: "There's no question
of the death sentence being lifted just because the judge
who passed the sentence has died. It will stand."

7 June 1989: Day 114
In Tehran for Ayatollah Khomeini's funeral, Dr Kalim
Siddiqui says that Salman Rushdie should withdraw his
book from sale and give the proceeds to a trust for the families of victims who died protesting against the novel in
Pakistan and India earlier in the year. "If this happened,
things could move forward very rapidly and you would see
full diplomatic relations restored within three to six
months," he says after talks with senior Iranian leaders.
"Iran has no intention of killing Mr Rushdie. It will not
withdraw the death threat, but is prepared to let the matter
drop," he adds.

8 June 1989: Day 115
A demand by French Muslims for the banning of *The
Satanic Verses* is refused in Paris, on the grounds that it is
impossible to ban a book which has not yet been published.

15 June 1989: Day 122
Venezuela bans *The Satanic Verses*.

20 June 1989: Day 127
Abdul Hussain Choudhury, a Muslim scholar and member
of the British Muslim Action Front, is given leave to appeal
in the High Court the Chief Metropolitan Magistrate's deci-

sion that the law of blasphemy applies only to Christianity.

22 June 1989: Day 129
Speaking in Moscow, Iranian President Ali Akbar Rafsanjani describes the threat to kill Mr Rushdie as one that has been endorsed by "the entire Muslim world" on the basis of the Shari'a (Islamic law), and adds: "What Ayatollah Ruhollah Khomeini said was a prescription of the Shari'a and not his personal opinion. There is no one in Iran who would want to, or could, take back that prescription."

23 June 1989: Day 130
At a public meeting in London to "Defend Salman Rushdie" speakers include Gita Saghal, Jasper Ridley, John Hoyland, Moochehr Mahjobi and Reza Marzban.

2 July 1989: Day 139
The first UK public reading of passages from *The Satanic Verses* is held in London at Conway Hall under the auspices of South Place Ethical Society.

4 July 1989: Day 141
Voices for Salman Rushdie present "An Unholy Night", a benefit for Salman Rushdie, featuring Kathy Acker, Manny Shirazi, Pauline Melville, Mehmet Yashin, Caryl Churchill, Hanif Kureishi, Jag Plah, Elizabeth Wilson, and "Hanging's Too Good For 'Em".

6 July 1989: Day 143
A firebomb attack on Collet's International Bookshop in London causes extensive damage.

19 July 1989: Day 156
The ICDSR holds a press conference at the Institute of Contemporary Arts in London to launch its publication, *Writers and Readers in Support of Salman Rushdie*, an updated edition of the *World Statement* signed by some 12,000 people from 67 countries. A message from Salman Rushdie acknowledges the substantial number of letters of support

147

he has received from Muslims and adds: "the process of mutual understanding within Islam will continue, leading to reconciliation".

The authorized French translation of *The Satanic Verses* is published by Christian Bourgeois, with the "support of the Ministère de la Culture et de la Communication de la République Française", and is endorsed by many publishing houses.

22 July 1989: Day 159
The Tribunal de Paris, chaired by M. Jean Favard, rules there is no case to seize or ban *The Satanic Verses*.

5 August 1989: Day 173
Muslims demonstrate in Leicester, UK, against *The Satanic Verses*.

3 September 1989: Day 202
A bomb left outside Liberty's department store in London, which is stocking *The Satanic Verses*, explodes, injuring an Irish tourist.

13 September 1989: Day 212
Penguin bookshops are attacked in York, Peterborough, Guildford and Nottingham.

26 September 1989: Day 225
First anniversary of the publication of *The Satanic Verses*. Viking/Penguin announce that 200,000 copies of the hardback edition have been sold in the UK.

10 October 1989: Day 239
The Frankfurt Book Fair opens. In an unprecedented gesture of support for Salman Rushdie, the organizers of the Book Fair exclude Iranian representation.

21 October 1989: Day 250
At a public meeting in Manchester, Dr Kalim Siddiqui invites the audience to raise hands in support of the *fatwa*

against Salman Rushdie, which results in shouts of "Death to Rushdie".

16 November 1989: Day 276
Crescent International, newspaper of the Muslim Institute, points out that "while the two million Muslims living in Britain should not kill Rushdie, the other 998 million Muslims in the world are free to do so if they can, when they can, where they can".

15 December 1989: Day 305
UK Day of Muslim Solidarity. It is claimed that at Friday prayers in mosques throughout the UK "as many as 300,000 Muslims" take part in shows of hand-raising in support of the death sentence on Salman Rushdie.

Merhdad Kokabi, an Iranian student at Manchester's Institute of Science and Technology, is charged with conspiracy to commit arson and cause explosions at bookshops selling *The Satanic Verses*.

7 January 1990: Day 328
Five hundred university students join demonstrators in front of the British Embassy in Tehran calling for the immediate release of Iranian student Merhdad Kokabi.

8 January 1990: Day 329
Muslims begin a five-day vigil outside the London headquarters of Viking/Penguin, publishers of *The Satanic Verses*.

14 January 1990: Day 335
The *Sunday Times* publishes the results of a survey of 100 bookshops showing that 57 think that Penguin should publish a paperback version of *The Satanic Verses*, 27 think it should not and 16 do not know.

21 January 1990: Day 342
Dr Kalim Siddiqui, addressing a Coventry convention held by the International Muslims Organization announces: "We have already gone as far as we can ever go to have *The*

Satanic Verses affair amicably settled." He adds: "If the book is withdrawn and compensation paid to the worst sufferers of this episode, we would consider the matter closed. If this offer is spurned, Muslims will pursue the author, the publishers, the distributors and the libraries for as long as it may be necessary."

29 January 1990: Day 350
The Director of Public Prosecutions announces that there is insufficient evidence to justify a prosecution over a speech given by Dr Kalim Siddiqui in Manchester in October 1989, when Dr Siddiqui had been alleged to solicit or incite the murder of Salman Rushdie.

4 February 1990: Day 356
Salman Rushdie breaks silence with an article, "In Good Faith", in the *Independent on Sunday*. He denies that he has committed blasphemy and states emphatically that he is not a Muslim.

5 February 1990: Day 357
Salman Rushdie urges Viking/Penguin to release the paperback edition of *The Satanic Verses*. Shabbir Akhtar, a member of the Bradford Council of Mosques, is quoted as stating: "If Rushdie cancels the paperback and engages in dialogue with people he has thus far dismissed, there is still scope for reconciliation."

6 February 1990: Day 358
The Herbert Read memorial lecture, *Is Nothing Sacred?*, written by Salman Rushdie, is read by Harold Pinter at the Institute of Contemporary Arts in London.

8 February 1990: Day 360
Nine Iranians suspected of plotting to murder Salman Rushdie are deported "for reasons of national security" because the activities of the nine are "not conducive to the public good", a Home Office spokesman says.

9 February 1990: Day 361
At a prayer meeting in Tehran, Iran's spiritual leader, Ayatollah Ali Khamenei reiterates the *fatwa* calling for the death of Salman Rushdie: "Imam Khomeini's decree about the author of the blasphemous book *The Satanic Verses* remains in force and must be implemented."

11 February 1990: Day 363
In the UK, the Islamic Society for the Promotion of Religious Tolerance unequivocally condemns Iran's reiteration of the death sentence on Salman Rushdie and offers a solution to the controversy surrounding *The Satanic Verses*: Mr Rushdie should accept that a "health warning" should be placed on the cover of the book which could emphasize that it was a work of fiction rather than "historical fact". In addition, a right of reply essay could be included in further editions of the novel. The society's chairman, Dr Hesham El-Essawy, says the reaffirmation of the death sentence is against the teaching of the Qur'an: "We call upon the leadership of Iran to state publicly that they will not engage in cross-border war-like actions such as employing a hit squad. We also call on them to distance themselves from the gangster movie tactics of bounty hunting," he says.

13 February 1990: Day 365
At a press conference at the Foreign Correspondents' Club in Tokyo to launch the Japanese translation of *The Satanic Verses*, its Italian publisher, Gianni Palma, is attacked with a microphone stand. The attacker, identified as Adnan Rashid, a Pakistani, is arrested and led away shouting Islamic prayers. A man identifying himself as a leader of the Pakistani community in Japan declares that Gianni Palma "cannot be allowed to live". Mr Palma says: "I am fighting for freedom of expression and I believe there are Japanese who want to read this book."

14 February 1990: Day 366
The ICDSR issues a *World Writers' Restatement* in defence of Salman Rushdie and free speech on the anniversary of the

proclamation of the *fatwa*. One hundred eminent writers around the world, including eight exiled Iranians, restate the principle that it is the right of all people to express their ideas and beliefs and to discuss them with their critics on the basis of mutual tolerance, free from censorship, intimidation and violence.

16 February 1990: Day 368
Mir Lohi, Commander-in-Chief of the Iranian Revolutionary Guard, states that they are ready to execute the death sentence against Salman Rushdie.

Yaqub Zaki (also known as James Dickie), of the Muslim Institute in London, refers to Salman Rushdie, in *Crescent International*, as a "coffee-coloured, lily-livered freak".

18 February 1990: Day 370
Dr Kalim Siddiqui addresses a rally in a London hall adorned with posters of Salman Rushdie which are inscribed: "Wanted dead or alive".

19 February 1990: Day 371
In the House of Lords, members raise questions concerning threats to the life of Salman Rushdie. The Lord Chancellor reveals that: "In the past year, the DPP has considered 39 complaints in respect of five instances of alleged threats to the life of Mr Rushdie.... In respect of each instance the director decided after very careful consideration that there was insufficient evidence to justify the institution of criminal proceedings."

Muhammad Yazdi, head of the Iranian judiciary, declares that Muslims who possess the means to kill Salman Rushdie, but do not do so, are sinners in the eyes of God.

25 February 1990: Day 377
Hazrat Mirza Tahir Ahmad, leader of the 10 million-strong Ahmadiyya Muslim community, condemns the *fatwa* against Salman Rushdie and his publishers.

27 February 1990: Day 379
Iran bans *Der Spiegel* for "insulting the sanctities of the Iranian people" as well as the late leader, Ayatollah Khomeini, and for its "hostile" stance on the *fatwa.*

4 March 1990: Day 384
In Thailand, some 200 Muslims burn an effigy of Salman Rushdie to protest against the Japanese translation of *The Satanic Verses.*

24 March 1990: Day 404
At the first national conference of the Muslim Youth Movement in Bradford a 16-year-old girl publicly calls for the stoning of Salman Rushdie saying: "He has humiliated and degraded us."

9 April 1990: Day 420
Appeals to reverse the refusal by magistrates to grant summonses against Salman Rushdie and his publishers for offences against Section 4(1) of the Public Order Act 1986, Seditious Libel, and Blasphemous Libel, are dismissed by the High Court.

28 April 1990: Day 439
Salman Rushdie, speaking on BBC radio, expresses surprise that no one has been prosecuted for "threats against him".

8th May 1990: Day 449
In a Gallup Poll published in the *Daily Telegraph*, the majority of respondents feel that Salman Rushdie should apologize for *The Satanic Verses.*

24th May 1990: Day 465
The High Court refuses the British Muslim Action Front leave to appeal to the House of Lords against the judgement that the law of blasphemy applies only to Christianity.

26th May 1990: Day 467
Five hundred youths march through Bradford city centre to

demonstrate against *The Satanic Verses*. The demonstration erupts into violence and sixteen youths are arrested.

28th May 1990: Day 469
A senior pro-Iranian Lebanese figure, Hussein Musawi, Head of Islamic Amal, says some British hostages held in Lebanon might be freed if Britain expels Salman Rushdie.

3 June 1990: Day 475
Senior Iranian Foreign Ministry official, Hussein Musavian, declares: "Nobody can revoke or amend the *fatwa* of the Imam Khomeini; it cannot be modified."

5 June 1990: Day 477
Application is to be made to issue in the UK a video of *International Guerillas*, a three-hour-long film which is breaking box-office records in Pakistan. The film's plot is based upon the exploits of three Pakistani warriors who have sworn to seek out and kill Salman Rushdie, who is depicted as an anti-Islamic, drunken, sadistic murderer, hiding on a Pacific island protected by hundreds of Israeli soldiers. The ICDSR states: "if the film does not infringe any laws, such as those on incitement to murder or racial hatred, then the Committee is opposed to any censorship of it."

On BBC *Newsnight*, Yaqub Zaki (James Dickie), of the Muslim Institute in London, expresses a wish for a hit squad to come from Iran to murder Salman Rushdie.

6 June 1990: Day 478
At a news conference in Tehran, Iranian President Ali Akbar Hashemi Rafsanjani says there is no possibility of lifting the *fatwa* condemning Salman Rushdie to death.

7 June 1990: Day 479
In a meeting with Frances D'Souza, Chairperson ICDSR, Mr William Waldegrave, Minister of State at the Foreign Office, reveals that, at a meeting between senior UK government officials and their Iranian counterparts, an agreement was reached that the Iranian government would neither encour-

age nor allow the implementation of the *fatwa*.

27 June 1990: Day 499
The Iranian government dismisses Salman Rushdie's offer
of financial help to Iranian earthquake victims.

14 July 1990: Day 516
In London, Dr Kalim Siddiqui tells a conference held by the
Muslim Institute: "the existence of a political and judicial
authority of Islam outside Britain has made us invincible".
The conference discusses Dr Kalim Siddiqui's recently
launched pamphlets, *The Muslim Manifesto* and *Declaration
on the Rushdie Affair*, which uphold the death sentence
imposed on Salman Rushdie and vote to mount a "campaign of civil disobedience" if all copies of *The Satanic Verses*
are not immediately withdrawn.

25 July 1990: Day 527
Article 19 protests the British Board of Film Classification's
refusal to grant a certificate to *International Guerillas* .

4 August 1990: Day 537
The 19th Islamic Foreign Ministers Conference adopts a
mandatory resolution calling on all member states to take
all necessary steps, including economic sanctions, against
the publisher of *The Satanic Verses* and its holding company.

17 August 1990: Day 550
The ban on *International Guerillas* is lifted after a statement
from Salman Rushdie urging that the film be shown so that
people could recognize it "for the distorted, incompetent
piece of trash that it is". The author writes: "I am opposed
in principle to the use of the archaic criminal laws of blasphemy, sedition and criminal libel against creative works."
He adds that he does not want "the dubious protection of
censorship", and will not seek or support any prosecution.

19 August 1990: Day 552
A firebomb is thrown at a public library in Lancashire.

6 September 1990: Day 570
Nadine Gordimer writes to Dr Ali Ahani, Ambassador of
Iran in France, enclosing an appeal to the government of
Iran, signed by a number of eminent people, including the
Presidents of Czechoslovakia and Lithuania, the French
Minister of Culture and members of governments, writers,
academics and others who attended a meeting in Oslo in
late August, asking that the appeal be forwarded to
President Rafsanjani. The appeal urges the government of
Iran to revoke the edict against Mr Rushdie's life and the
offer of bounty money.

10 September 1990: Day 574
The President of the EC Council, Italian Foreign Minister
Gianni de Michelis, announces that the European
Community believes it is close to an exchange of letters
which could lead to the lifting of the *fatwa*.

27 September 1990: Day 591
Partial diplomatic relations between the UK and Iran are
restored after assurances from the Iranian government that
Salman Rushdie's alleged blasphemy against Islam will now
be regarded as a religious matter and there will be no interference in Britain's internal affairs. The *fatwa* will not be
dropped, but Iran gives assurances that the death sentence
will not be carried out at the behest of the Iranian government. The question as to whether individual Muslims are
bound by that decision is left open.

30 September 1990: Day 594
Salman Rushdie is interviewed by Melvyn Bragg on ITV's
The South Bank Show, his first television appearance since
the *fatwa* was pronounced.

3 November 1990: Day 628
The Iranian Embassy reopens in London.

26 November 1990: Day 651
Salman Rushdie, appearing on BBC2's *The Late Show* in an

interview with Michael Ignatieff, says: "I am talking with Muslim leaders to try to find common ground. There is a lot of common ground and the point is to try to make it more solid."

27 November 1990: Day 652
UK Muslim leaders refute claims by Salman Rushdie that he has been in negotiations with Muslim leaders.

24 December 1990: Day 679
Salman Rushdie meets with a group of influential Muslims, including the Egyptian Minister of Religious Affairs, and disavows any statements by characters in his novel that insult the Islamic faith; promises not to permit further translations of his novel in paperback while any risk of further offence exists; agrees to "embrace Islam"; and pledges to "continue to work for a better understanding of Islam".

25 December 1990: Day 680
The Iranian News Agency quotes the newspaper *Jomhuri Eslamias* as saying: "If Rushdie's repentance and his return to Islam is seen as a sign of his bravery, naturally it is necessary that he show greater bravery and prepare himself for death."

26 December 1990: Day 681
Dr Hesham El-Essawy, Chairman of the Islamic Society for the Promotion of Religious Tolerance, sends telex messages to Ayatollah Ali Khamenei and Iranian President Rafsanjani, calling for Iranians to show the "forgiving and merciful nature of Islam".

27 December 1990: Day 682
Ayatollah Ali Khamenei declares that the *fatwa* is irrevocable and will remain in place even if Salman Rushdie "becomes the most pious man of his time".
   In an interview on American television, Salman Rushdie says he is "beginning to get a little disturbed by the lack of reaction on the part of the British government to renewed

threats from abroad".

28 December 1990: Day 683

Salman Rushdie appeals to Iran to show an understanding of his work and lift the death sentence against him.

In an article in *The Times* entitled "Why I Have Embraced Islam", Salman Rushdie states: "A man's spiritual choices are a matter of conscience, arrived at after deep reflection and in the privacy of his heart." He says that he has been "finding my own way towards an intellectual understanding of religion, and religion for me has always meant Islam. I am certainly not a good Muslim. But I am able now to say that I am Muslim; in fact it is a source of happiness to say that I am now inside, and a part of, the community whose values have always been closest to my heart." Writing on the question of the withdrawal of his novel Mr Rushdie says: "I have agreed not to permit new translations of *The Satanic Verses*, nor to publish an English-language paperback edition, while any risk of further offence remains.... I believe the book must continue to be available, so that it can gradually be seen for what it is. I will be discussing with Penguin Books the possibility of adding to the existing hardback editions a statement declaring that it is not intended as an attack on Islam."

29 December 1990: Day 684

The UK Action Committee on Islamic Affairs states that Salman Rushdie's "embrace of Islam" is a ploy to get him "off the hook" and vows to continue its campaign until the book is totally withdrawn and an unqualified apology is tendered to Muslims and payment of damages is made to an Islamic charity.

30 December 1990: Day 685

On BBC Radio 4's *Moral Maze*, Dr Kalim Siddiqui says Salman Rushdie has been "found guilty of a capital offence in the eyes of the highest legal authority in Islam and what is left is the application of that punishment". In an *Independent on Sunday* interview, Dr Siddiqui says that

Salman Rushdie should "pay with his life" for *The Satanic Verses*.

31 December 1990: Day 686
Speaking on BBC Radio 4's *Sunday* programme, Salman Rushdie says he has received blessings from Egyptian officials and scholars and an invitation to meet Sheikh Gad el-Haq Ali Gad el-Haq, the Supreme Mufti, of al-Azhar in Cairo.

6 January 1991: Day 692
Speaking from a secret location on a phone-in programme broadcast by two Asian radio stations in Britain, Salman Rushdie says that Muslims would be committing a crime against God if they tried to kill him. Insisting that he has returned to the Islamic faith, he says: "When a Muslim murders another Muslim it is not a religious act, it's murder. It's not my immortal soul that would be in danger, it's his." Mr Rushdie says he is not prepared to withdraw his book: "I think I have done a great deal, stopping the publication of the paperback edition and saying I wouldn't permit further translations." The author welcomes a radio station poll which claims that 90 per cent of callers feel he should be forgiven.

A moderate Muslim organization is launched to isolate the fanatical fringe among Britain's 1.5 million Muslims and resolve the Salman Rushdie issue. Islamic scholar Zaki Badawi, principal of the Muslim College in London, who has condemned Mr Rushdie's alleged blasphemy but deplored his persecution, says that he is determined to rally moderate opinion.

In Tehran, Hojatoleslam Ahmad Khomeini, son of the late Ayatollah Khomeini, says that Britain will face unspecified reprisals unless it frees Merhdad Kokabi, awaiting trial in the UK on arson and bombing charges.

7 January 1991: Day 693
Merhdad Kokabi goes on trial at the Old Bailey, charged with conspiracy to commit arson and cause explosions at

bookshops selling *The Satanic Verses* during the spring and autumn of 1989.

8 January 1991: Day 694
Publishers Viking/Penguin come under increasing pressure from Muslims to make conciliatory moves to match Salman Rushdie's offer to abandon the paperback edition and embrace Islam. The British Muslim Forum, a new body aiming to improve the image Islam has acquired since the Rushdie affair, believes Viking/Penguin should say it will print no more editions of the book. Bob Gregory, spokesman for the publishers, says that any decisions about the future of the book would have to be taken after a discussion with Mr Rushdie.

15 January 1991: Day 701
Salman Rushdie goes into deeper hiding in response to renewed threats to implement the *fatwa* against him.

14 February 1991: Day 731
Statement from the ICDSR on the second anniversary of the *fatwa* against Salman Rushdie notes that the death threat has been renewed many times by ministers of the Iranian government and that, since the resumption of diplomatic relations with Iran in September 1990, the UK government has remained silent on the renewed death threats.

2 March 1991: Day 747
Iranian religious leaders and scholars participating in an international conference of Muslim leaders in Tehran warn that the *fatwa* is "irrevocable" and renew calls for the swift implementation of the death sentence on Rushdie.

5 March 1991: Day 750
Hassani Sanei of the 15 Khordad Foundation, doubles the reward to US$2 million for any associate, relative or neighbour killing Salman Rushdie.

The European Commission of Human Rights declares inadmissible Abdul Hussain Choudhury's application alleging interference with freedom of religion, and upholds the ruling that protection against blasphemy in the UK does not extend to Islam.

12 March 1991: Day 757
Charges against Merhdad Kokabi of conspiracy to commit arson and cause explosions at bookshops selling *The Satanic Verses* are dropped at the High Court in London, but his deportation is recommended. Judge Kenneth Richardson says he bases his decision purely on the administration of justice. He had heard that nine Iranians who had flown to Britain to give defence evidence had been so intimidated by Heathrow immigration officials that they caught the next flight back to Iran and refused to return. The UK Home Office denies that there had been intimidation of witnesses and says a deportation order against Mr Kokabi will remain in force despite the dropping of the charges.

15 March 1991: Day 760
Merhdad Kokabi is deported from the UK and arrives in Tehran to a hero's welcome led by a cabinet minister and several MPs. Kokabi urges well-wishers to stay loyal to the "sacred ideals" of the late Ayatollah Khomeini and states that Salman Rushdie should be killed. It is reported that Merhdad Kokabi has been appointed as special adviser to the Iranian government in the Science Ministry and will be responsible for the placement of Iranian students abroad.

6 April 1991: Day 782
Writers participating in New Zealand Writers' Week sign a petition, calling upon world leaders to continue to repudiate the *fatwa* against Salman Rushdie and his publishers.

3 May 1991: Day 809
Two London Central Mosque Imams read a statement saying that Salman Rushdie's conversion to Islam cannot be accepted because he has not completely withdrawn *The Satanic Verses*. Sheikh Gamal Manna Solaiman and Sheikh Hamed Khalifa both witnessed Mr Rushdie's embrace of

Islam at a meeting on 24 December 1990 and, although they regard his book as offensive, they encouraged the Muslim community to accept Mr Rushdie's conversion. Since December, neither Imam has been able to lead the Friday prayers without encountering violent protests from some worshippers.

9 May 1991: Day 815
Salman Rushdie writes to the *Independent* claiming that Sheikhs Gamal and Hamed have been intimidated by "bully-boy tactics used against them in recent months", and that such intimidation has been a feature of this affair from the beginning "and must be resisted".

13 May 1991: Day 819
Dr Hesham El-Essawy, Chairman for the Islamic Society for the Promotion of Religious Tolerance, who witnessed Mr Rushdie's embrace of Islam, says the Imams had agreed to retract their previous statements under "tremendous pressure from a fanatical minority".

20 May 1991: Day 826
In Australia, Iranian Foreign Minister Ali Akbar Velayati states: "This is an Islamic issue and it concerns Islamic values. After that book was published and the great leader of the revolution had issued his decree, the issue was discussed by the Islamic Conference Organization in Riyadh and all Muslim countries unanimously endorsed the decree on Rushdie's apostasy. This indicates that what he did was against the beliefs of one billion Muslims, not against Iran."

1 June 1991: Day 838
John R. MacArthur addresses the American Booksellers Association Convention in New York and argues for the publication of an English-language paperback edition of *The Satanic Verses*.

3 July 1991: Day 870
Milan: Ettore Capriolo, 61, Italian translator of *The Satanic*

Verses, is beaten and repeatedly stabbed by a man claiming to be Iranian, who demands Salman Rushdie's address. Ettore Capriolo translated the book in 1989 for the Mondadori publishing house and had been given police protection for several months during 1990 after receiving threats from Islamic fundamentalists.

11 July 1991: Day 878
Tokyo: Professor Hitoshi Igarashi, Japanese translator of *The Satanic Verses,* is stabbed to death at Tsukuba University. A spokesman for the Pakistan Association in Japan says: "the murder was completely, 100 per cent connected with the book. ... Today we have been congratulating each other. Everyone was really happy."

12 July 1991: Day 879
Salman Rushdie issues a statement: "I am extremely distressed by the news of the murder of Mr Hitoshi Igarashi, and I offer my condolences and deepest sympathy to his family. Only a few days ago, Mr Ettore Capriolo, the Italian translator of *The Satanic Verses,* narrowly survived a similar, horrifying attack. It is hard to avoid linking the two events. The crisis created by the Iranian *fatwa* of February 1989 has faded from the news of late; indeed it has been more or less impossible to interest the British news media in the continued threat. In spite of this silence, however, the danger to all those named in the *fatwa* has, if anything, increased. It has been suggested (by, amongst others, the British government) that the only thing to be done about the *fatwa* is to let it fade quietly away over a period of time. The murder of Mr Igarashi and the stabbing of Mr Capriolo show us that this approach simply will not work. I therefore appeal to the British, Italian and Japanese governments, as well as all leaders of the world comunity, Muslim and non-Muslim alike, to make urgent representations to the government of Iran. International law, humanitarian principles and the essentially merciful character of Islam itself all require that the *fatwa* be set aside before any more innocent people die."
UK Minister of State Douglas Hogg writes to PEN

American Center saying that to press loudly for the *fatwa* to be lifted would in the UK government's view be a mistake and reduce chances of securing the release of British and other hostages.

14 July 1991: Day 881
Liaqat Hussain, President of Bradford's Council of Mosques, says: "These people who have translated cannot get away with it. That is the position. There will be repercussions. Even if it means death."

18 July 1991: Day 885
The Japan PEN Club issues a statement following the murder of Professor Igarashi: "If this atrocity is connected with the translation of this book, it would be a grave threat to the freedom of expression set forth in the Charter of the International PEN and a fearful violation of basic human rights. If this atrocious crime was committed for such a reason, it cannot be tolerated, regardless of any consideration of religious differences, and the Japan PEN Club, as an organization devoted to promoting mutual understanding among different cultures, expresses its deep sorrow and sincere condolences on the tragic death of Professor Igarashi".

23 July 1991: Day 890
The People's Mojahedin of Iran holds a London press conference and claims it has a tape recording of a telephone conversation, between an Iranian official in President Rafsanjani's office and another, which refers openly to the assassination of Professor Igarashi and the assassination attempt on the Italian translator. The group also claims that death squads have been despatched from Iran to Italy, Japan, France, Switzerland, Germany, Canada, Nigeria and Algeria.

The ICDSR issues a press release welcoming the United States government's decision to veto the £90 million sale of British civilian aircraft to Iran, and reiterating the Committee's belief that international pressure of this kind is an essential prerequisite to halting illegal and terrorist attempts to kill Salman Rushdie.

26 July 1991: Day 893
The Canadian *Globe and Mail* publishes an article by
Nazneen Sadiq condemning the inaction of governments
championing the cause of human rights who sanction "a
regime that is undeniably linked to a group of people who
hire mercenary killers". The article calls on Islamic scholars
and theologians to "come out of hiding", and asks "... why
haven't the moderates of the Sunni sect of Islam made the
Shi'ite exploitation of the religious decree a point of vigorous debate in the Islamic conferences that assemble in
Middle Eastern cities?"

15 September 1991: Day 944
Salman Rushdie receives a Writers' Guild award for his children's book, *Haroun and the Sea of Stories*. Escorted by
Special Branch bodyguards, he makes a brief appearance at
the ceremony in London and, in an address to the audience, describes the past two years and seven months since
the *fatwa* was pronounced. He earns a standing ovation
when he says: "I hope that you'll continue to support me. I
hope that you will continue your work and make it clear
that we will not get used to the idea that a man may be murdered for a book."

22 September 1991: Day 951
The Phalangist Radio Free Lebanon reports that Islamic
Amal movement leader Hussein Musawi has said that
Salman Rushdie's recent literary award will delay the
hostage release process, and adds that the group is commit-
ted to Imam Khomeini's ruling to kill the author.

26 September 1991: Day 955
The organizers of the Frankfurt Book Fair withdraw invita-
tions to Iranian publishers after pressure from German publishers, authors and politicians who say their presence is
incompatible with the continuing death threat against
Salman Rushdie.

30 September 1991: Day 959
Iran bans German publishers from attending the Tehran
International Book Fair.

28 October 1991: Day 987
At a press conference launching moves to set up a 200-seat
Muslim National Council in Britain, Dr Kalim Siddiqui says
that the Rushdie affair is "dead and buried".

6 November 1991: Day 996
A vigil in London, organized by friends of Salman Rushdie,
to mark the author's 1,000th day in hiding, is cancelled after
a warning from the Foreign Office that the event might
jeopardize an early release of Terry Waite and other
Western hostages held in Beirut. The author had asked his
supporters to forgo the demonstration: "not in deference to
the Foreign Office but rather as an effort to clean up the
mess they have made. There is only one reason for making
this choice, and his name is Terry Waite. The bad faith lies
in the Foreign Office's abandonment of the position that it
ought never to trade in human rights. It now appears to
have taken the position that the rights of those named in
the *fatwa* are to be sacrificed."

11 November 1991: Day 1001
US PEN, supported by the Fund for Free Expression,
Article 19, *Harpers'* Magazine, Jack Mapange, Norman
Mailer and Faith Sale, holds a demonstration at Dag
Hammarskjöld Plaza, New York, to mark the thousandth
day of the *fatwa* against Salman Rushdie. Letters of protest
are handed to the US Mission to the United Nations and to
UN Secretary-General, Javier Perez de Cuellar.
  Friends of Salman Rushdie, including Caroline Michel,
Melvyn Bragg, Harold Pinter, Alan Yentob and Martin
Amis, who reluctantly cancelled their proposed London
vigil, hold a public reading of letters of support for the
author at Waterstone's bookshop in Charing Cross Road.
Statements include those from party leaders Neil Kinnock
and Paddy Ashdown, CSFR President Vaclav Havel, and

Nobel Laureate Nadine Gordimer.

In a UK *Independent* article, Ziauddin Sardar advises Salman Rushdie that the threat to him can never be banished; that since he has chosen to keep *The Satanic Verses* in print, he must live in its shadow: "Under such circumstances, the best course for Mr Rushdie and his supporters is to shut up. The more notice Mr Rushdie draws to his plight, the more he will be exposed to the attention of some frustrated subcontinental Muslim whose own ontological plight and powerlessness can be resolved only through the barrel of a gun. A fly caught in a cobweb does not draw attention to itself; it lies motionless in the hope that the spider will find some other distraction."

18 November 1991: Day 1008
Hostages Terry Waite and Tom Sutherland are released.

22 November 1991: Day 1012
Dr Carey, Archbishop of Canterbury, condemns Salman Rushdie's "outrageous slur" on the Prophet Muhammad in *The Satanic Verses* and says: "Tolerance is achieved when people hold their religion as so important that to part from it is to die, and at the same time realize that another person's values are just as important and as real."

24 November 1991: Day 1014
On BBC radio, Salman Rushdie says that Britain should not normalize relations with Iran while the *fatwa* against him remains in force and calls on the Archbishop of Canterbury to appeal to Iranian religious leaders for an end to the death sentence.

The *Sunday Telegraph* leader criticizes the Archbishop of Canterbury: "Dr Carey may be willing to die for the Ayatollahs' right to believe. But it is Mr Rushdie who is under an Islamic sentence of death, and English law would call his killing murder. Yet Dr Carey made no criticism of the *fatwa*. His defence of others' beliefs must include the beliefs of Mr Rushdie. If the Archbishop lacks the intellect to distinguish between freedom of conscience and freedom to commit crimes he should keep quiet."

12 December 1991: Day 1032

In the US, amid stringent security, Salman Rushdie address-es a meeting to commemorate the 200th anniversary of the Bill of Rights, as a guest of the graduate school of journal-ism at Colombia University. Referring to his meeting with Muslim scholars on Christmas Eve 1990, he says: "Those who were surprised and displeased by what I did perhaps failed to see that I wanted to make peace between the war-ring halves of the world, which were also the warring halves of my soul.... I have never disowned my book, nor regretted writing it. I said I was sorry to have offended people, because I had not set out to do so, and so I am.... Indeed, the chief benefit of my meeting with the six Islamic schol-ars... was that they agreed that the novel had no insulting motives. 'In Islam, it is a man's intention that counts,' I was told. 'Now we will launch a worldwide campaign on your behalf to explain that there has been a great mistake.' In this context I agreed to suspend – not cancel – a paperback edition to create 'space for reconciliation'. Alas, I overesti-mated these men. Within days, all but one of them had broken their promises and recommenced to vilify me and my work.... The suspension of the paperback began to look like a surrender. In the aftermath of the attacks on my translators, it looks even more craven. It has now been more than three years since *The Satanic Verses* was pub-lished; that's a long, long 'space for reconciliation'. Long enough. I accept I was wrong to have given way on this point. *The Satanic Verses* must be freely available and easily affordable if only because, if it is not read, these years will have no meaning. Those who forget the past are con-demned to repeat it.... 'Free speech is a non-starter,' says one of my Islamic extremist opponents. No, sir, it is not. Free speech is the whole thing, the whole ball game. Free speech is life itself."

13 December 1991: Day 1033

During the 6th Islamic Organization Conference in Dakar,

the *fatwa* against Rushdie is confirmed.

17 December 1992: Day 1037
In a UK *Guardian* article, "Foundered on Bad Faith", Dr Hesham El-Essawy, chairman of the Islamic Society for the Promotion of Religious Tolerance, and a member of the group of Islamic scholars who met with Salman Rushdie in December 1990, accuses the author of an insincere return to Islam and of reneging on the agreement they made to defuse the *fatwa* crisis. Claiming that 95 per cent of Muslims had welcomed Mr Rushdie back into the fold as a result of the scholars' efforts, Dr El-Essawy claims that the author "did not discharge his side of our agreement".

18 December 1991: Day 1038
Salman Rushdie writes to the *Guardian* refuting Dr El-Essawy's allegations, and claims that the Islamic scholars, "as a matter of public record", quickly joined the campaign to have *The Satanic Verses* withdrawn altogether. "Our dialogue broke down after he, too, attacked me in print, accusing me of cowardice and the like."

20 December 1991: Day 1040
The UK trade magazine, *The Bookseller*, calls for the publication of a paperback edition of *The Satanic Verses* and argues that the novel should be accessible to a larger audience so that there be a more widely informed opinion. The editorial claims that the publication of a paperback has less to do with the principle of freedom to publish than it has with the question of how best to respond to threats of terrorism, and urges a consortium of publishers to undertake publication so that the burden of responsibility should not be undertaken by Viking/Penguin.

25 December 1991: Day 1045
In Egypt, writer Alaa Hamed is sentenced to eight years' imprisonment and fined 2,500 Egyptian pounds. His novel, *A Distance in a Man's Mind*, is judged to constitute a threat to "national unity" and to "social peace". His publisher,

Mohammed Madbouli, and printer, Fathi Abu al-Fadi, receive similar sentences. The Islamic Research Academy of al-Azhar had reported the book to the public prosecutor's office; the author was arrested on 12 March 1990 and his novel was confiscated. The grounds for the arrest and confiscation were that the novel contained subversive opinions about religion in general and Islam in particular.

11 January 1992: Day 1061
At the Cairo International Book Fair, religious censors from al-Azhar University seize eight publications on Islamic themes, some of which had been published for as long as 12 years. One of the writers whose work is seized is Mohammed Sa'ed Ashmawi, a Chief Justice of the Martial State Security Court.

28 January 1992: Day 1078
The German newspaper *die tageszeitung* launches a campaign of letters to Salman Rushdie to mark the approaching third anniversary of the pronouncement of the *fatwa* against the author. The campaign is taken up by newspapers in twenty-two other countries.

In New York, a consortium of publishers, writers and human rights groups, under the auspices of the Authors' Guild, announce they will publish an English-language paperback edition of *The Satanic Verses* in the spring.

31 January 1992: Day 1081
Iqbal Sacranie, convenor of the UK Action Committee on Islamic Affairs, announces that the decision to publish the paperback version of *The Satanic Verses* is highly insensitive and will "only further aggravate the deep hurt caused to Muslims".

13 February 1992: Day 1094
Iranian newspapers *Abrar* and *Jomhouri-Eslami*, describing the death sentence against Salman Rushdie as "a divine command to stone the devil to death", call on Muslims worldwide to execute the British author. In a special supple-

ment, *Jomhouri-Eslami* publishes extracts of statements from Iranian leaders of all political and religious views who, it says, support the death sentence on Salman Rushdie.

115 MEPs, drawn from all twelve European Community member states, sign a resolution in the European Parliament in Strasbourg in support of Salman Rushdie which "recalls that the third anniversary of the issue of the *fatwa* falls tomorrow,... expresses deep sympathy for the continuing difficulties experienced by the author and calls upon all member states to press the Iranian authorities to withdraw the death threat".

14 February 1992: Day 1095

In London, ICDSR members and friends of Salman Rushdie lay a heart of roses beneath a plaque commemorating those executed for heresy in the 15th and 16th centuries: "In tribute to all those around the world who struggle courageously to exercise their right to freedom of expression and to defend the right of others, in the face of crushing censorship, intolerance and public silence."

Representatives of the ICDSR and Article 19 meet with senior officials at the Iranian Embassy. The delegation emphasizes that the removal of the bounty is an essential first step to deter contract killers, amongst others. The Iranian officials deny any government connection with the 15 Khordad Foundation. The delegation specifically requests that its concerns be conveyed to the Chargé d'Affaires and to the government in Iran, and that the Committee be kept informed of any developments. The Iranian officials agree to do so. No restrictions of confidentiality are placed on the meeting and it is hoped that further meetings will take place.

Friends of Salman Rushdie host an event in London entitled *What is to be Done? – Three Years of the Fatwa.* Speakers include Günter Grass, Tom Stoppard and Martin Amis with additional videoed statements by Edward Saïd, Nadine Gordimer, Seamus Heaney and Derek Walcott. Salman Rushdie makes an unannounced appearance at the event, to tremendous applause, and states: "Three years of menaces is a very, very long time. I refuse to be an unperson. I refuse to forgo the right to publish my work." The lecture is broadcast by BBC2 TV.

In Australia, the Free Speech Committee, together with the Library Society of New South Wales, the Australian Society of Authors, the Australian Book Publishers' Association and the Australian Writers' Guild hold a public reading of Salman Rushdie's works at the State Library of New South Wales in Sydney.

In France, the Université Paris VII and the French League for Human Rights host a lecture by Carmel Bedford (Secretary ICDSR) on the subject of the *fatwa* and the campaign in defence of Salman Rushdie.

In Ireland, leading writers give a reading in solidarity with Salman Rushdie in Dublin's Writers' Museum. The initiative is supported by the writers', translators' and journalists' unions, and BBC Radio Ulster record the proceedings for a special Easter Sunday programme.

New Zealand PEN members hold a series of readings in Dunedin to mark the anniversary.

Swiss Roman PEN hosts a lecture entitled *Writers, Journalists and Human Rights*, chaired by Laurence Deonna, UNESCO Peace Education Prize winner.

16 February 1992: Day 1097

Danish PEN, in collaboration with *Politiken*, hosts a "Salman Rushdie Matinee" at the Folketeatret, Copenhagen, featuring actors, poets, playwrights and musicians. Danish TV transmits a one-hour news programme, including an interview with Rushdie.

PEN Center USA West initiates a letter writing campaign, and hosts a reading and discussion in support of Salman Rushdie.

17 February 1992: Day 1098

The Iranian Embassy in London issues a press release which states: "1. None of this Embassy's diplomats has had a meeting with the representative of the 'International Committee for the Defence of Salman Rushdie'. 2. In a letter dated 7

February 1992, Dr D'Souza requested a meeting with an Embassy official. In response to this request, it was agreed for Dr D'Souza to present her case to a local employee of the Embassy. 3. Following a discussion of human rights situation and the recent general amnesty for prisoners in the Islamic Republic of Iran, Dr D'Souza made a reference to the late Imam's *fatwa* relating to Salman Rushdie, author of *The Satanic Verses.* The reply she received may be summed up as follows: (a) Appropriate clarification was given with regard to human rights issues and the recent general amnesty in the Islamic Republic of Iran. (b) On the question of Salman Rushdie, it was reiterated that the *fatwa* is a global Islamic matter and absolutely irreversible. (c) The *fatwa* is a universal issue in the world of Islam and relates to a billion Muslims all over the world. (d) As a school of thought and practice, as a way of life, Islam has its own defence mechanism which emanates from within Islam itself. Therefore, it would be a pure fallacy to suggest that the *fatwa* may be withdrawn, now or at any time in the future. Any other interpretation of the above-mentioned meeting and its contents is categorically denied."

27 February 1992: Day 1108
A petition signed by 111 of Denmark's 189 MPs is handed over to the Iranian Ambassador to Denmark. The signatories, from all eight political parties, appeal to President Rafsanjani and his government to lift the *fatwa* against Salman Rushdie.

6 March 1992: Day 1116
A group of more than 300 writers from Denmark, Estonia, Finland, Germany, Latvia, Lithuania, Norway, Poland, Russia and Sweden, on board the ship *Konstantin Simonov*, send a message to Salman Rushdie: "We are writing to you from a unique reunion of writers from... countries whose intellectuals until now were prevented to meet in this way.... We are thinking of you... being forced to live in an unsupportable situation....We urge all governments and international bodies to act immediately and accordingly so that

your sentence will be abolished."

16 March 1992: Day 1126
Fifty exiled Iranian intellectuals and artists sign a declaration which states: "As this outrageous and deliberate attack on freedom of speech was issued in Iran, we feel that Iranian intellectuals should condemn this *fatwa* and defend Salman Rushdie more forcefully than any other group on earth.... We raise our voices unanimously in the defence of Salman Rushdie and remind the whole world that Iranian writers, artists, journalists and thinkers, inside Iran, are persistently under the merciless pressure of religious censorship and that the number of those who have been imprisoned or even executed there for 'blasphemy' is not negligible. We are convinced that any tolerance shown towards the systematic violation of human rights in Iran, cannot but encourage and embolden the Islamic regime to expand and export its terrorist ideas and methods worldwide."

24 March 1992: Day 1134
Salman Rushdie appears unannounced in Washington, at a meeting sponsored by the American University and the Freedom Forum, and launches the English-language paperback edition of *The Satanic Verses*, published by an anonymous consortium. He announces that a planned meeting with senior members of Congress and Senators on Capitol Hill has been abruptly cancelled. Interviewed on CBS News before the conference he says that the British government has indicated it will not be able to continue indefinitely with his expensive security.

25 March 1992: Day 1135
Salman Rushdie meets with members of the US Senate Foreign Relations Committee and appeals for pressure against Iran to lift the death sentence against him. Denying allegations that the Bush administration had pressured Congressional leaders into cancelling a meeting with Mr Rushdie, White House spokesman Marlin Fitzwater states:

"There is no reason for any special relationship with Rushdie... he's an author, he's here, he's doing interviews and book tours and things that authors do. But there's no reason for us to have any special interest in him.... He doesn't write about government policies." State Department spokeswoman Margaret Tutweiler says that no administration officials will meet with the author "because such a meeting could, and possibly might, be misinterpreted".

27 March 1992: Day 1137
The *New York Times* accuses the Bush administration of being cowed by the Iranian government. Commenting on the statements by the White House and State Department spokespersons the newspaper states: "This is sadly consistent with three years of official waffling ever since Ayatollah Khomeini denounced *The Satanic Verses* as blasphemous and called for the death of its author and publishers.... Far more than Mr Rushdie's life is at risk if Western states do not jointly warn Iran that it cannot win the trade it covets until it ceases exporting and exhorting terrorism."

8 April 1992: Day 1149
The English-language paperback edition of *The Satanic Verses*, imported from the US, goes on sale in the UK.

1 May 1992: Day 1172
In India, Muslim students protest against Professor Mushirul Hasan, historian, and Vice-Chancellor of the Jamia Millia Islamia University in Delhi, calling for him to be fired, and the university is forced to close indefinitely. Professor Hasan had said, in a magazine interview, that although Salman Rushdie's book had offended his Muslim sensibilities, everyone had a right to be heard.

2 May 1992: Day 1173
The Rt Hon Paddy Ashdown MP, leader of the UK Liberal Democratic Party, writes to Prime Minister John Major, expressing his concern that the withdrawal of police protection for Salman Rushdie is being considered.

Dr Kalim Siddiqui says that the *fatwa* on Salman Rushdie should be a deterrent to other writers and artists tempted to abuse Islam and adds that "the *fatwa* and our presence in this country will keep Rushdie pinned down in his bunker for the rest of his life. Keeping Rushdie in his rabbit hole is victory enough for us and our future generations."

6 May 1992: Day 1177
Playwright Arnold Wesker, in a letter to the UK *Guardian*, responds to Dr Kalim Siddiqui's threat: "He is a type not restricted to Islam. Siddiquis can be found, glued like barnacles to wrecked ships, in most religious and political ideologies. They hate and fear spirits, often embodied in the artist and intellectual, who will laugh at and question their pompous tenets. He continues to refer to *The Satanic Verses* as an offence to Islam. But threats to publishers, bombs planted in bookshops, attacks on people in public places caught reading the book, the abominable knifing and murder of two of the book's translators – these are greater offences."

13 May 1992: Day 1184
Japanese newspaper *Yukan Fuji* publishes a report which states: "authorities believe that three men, members of an Islamic extremist organization, are responsible for the assassination of Professor Igarashi". The report claims that the three travelled to Tokyo via the People's Republic of China.

15 May 1992: Day 1186
After pressure from students, politicians and other faculty members, Professor Mushirul Hasan, Vice-Chancellor of Jamia Millia Islamia University in Delhi, India, issues a statement which regrets his previous stance upholding Salman Rushdie's right to be read. Despite this, Jamia students are willing to let him teach only if he admits that death is Islam's punishment for blasphemy. The university remains closed.

22 May 1992: Day 1193
UK Prime Minister John Major's Private Secretary writes to the ICDSR: "Mr Rushdie will continue to receive protection while the threat to him remains at a level which requires it."

26 May 1992: Day 1197
In Japan, TBS broadcasts an interview with Salman Rushdie in which the author describes his feelings at the killing of Professor Igarashi. "It was disgusting that somebody who ... was a considerable scholar of Islam, who had written a number of books which were very sympathetic books, presenting Islam to the Japanese public, that such a man should be murdered was an appalling thing."

17 June 1992: Day 1219
The Iranian Press Agency reports that the 15 Khordad Foundation will also "cover expenses for the extermination of the cursed writer in addition to the US$2 million".

22 June 1992: Day 1224
Amidst stringent security, Danish PEN hosts a meeting in support of freedom of expression at the Louisiana Art Museum. Günter Grass introduces surprise guest Salman Rushdie saying: "If Salman Rushdie is a hostage so, too, are we."

23 June 1992: Day 1225
Salman Rushdie holds a press conference, on a boat off the coast of Denmark, and meets with ex-Prime Minister, Anker Jorgensen.

24 June 1992: Day 1226
Mark Fisher, Labour Shadow Minister for the Arts and Media, sponsors an all-party meeting with Salman Rushdie in the Grand Committee Room of the House of Commons. When asked what Europe can do, the author says that Iran needs the backing of Europe for its ambitions; that this is not a parochial issue; it is international and, therefore, requires an international response.

30 June 1992: Day 1232
A petition signed by 170 Iranian MPs states: "We deputies of the Majlis, in obedience to the decisive views of the eminent leader, His Eminence Ayatollah Khamenei, announce that the Imam's historic *fatwa* about the apostasy of Salman Rushdie remains in force as before, and that all Muslims and all the world's Hezbollah forces are duty-bound to carry it out." This is the first reference by the Iranian government to Hezbollah's involvement.

10 July 1992: Day 1242
In a statement on the anniversary of the death of Professor Hitoshi Igarashi, Salman Rushdie says: "I have come to understand that what is important is precisely *not to become accustomed to the intolerable.* In our modern world, with its rapid shifts of focus and its short attention span, it is all too easy to lose interest in a particular case, no matter how vivid the story once was. But to do so in this case would be an insult to Professor Igarashi's memory. It simply can never be acceptable to murder a man in the name of any god or ideology. In such a case, morality is never on the side of the murderers.

24 July 1992: Day 1256
Three Iranians – two employees at the Iranian Embassy in London and a student – are expelled from the UK; they are believed to have conspired to kill Salman Rushdie.

27 July 1992: Day 1259
Salman Rushdie appears with author Mario Vargas Llosa at a seminar entitled "The Novelist and his Phantoms" in Madrid. At the following press conference, Mario Vargas Llosa demands that the Spanish government intervene with Iran to bring an end to the *fatwa.*

19 August 1992: Day 1282
Salman Rushdie is guest of honour at a Norwegian PEN gathering at which more than 100 writers, academics and politicians are present, including Norway's Cultural

Minister. He also meets with representatives of the Nordic Council and senior politicians.

20 August 1992: Day 1283
Salman Rushdie meets with the Education Minister and is also a guest at a dinner hosted by Norway's representative to the European Commission of Human Rights.

21 August 1992: Day 1284
Salman Rushdie holds a tightly-guarded press conference in Oslo, after meeting with government ministers, and says: "I hope that this will be the beginning of pressure on Iran from another direction." He adds: "To remove the *fatwa* is part of the price of entering the civilized world [for Iran]."

8 September 1992: Day 1302
A three-week Novel of the Americas Symposium, convened by Professor Raymond L. Williams, opens at the University of Colorado at Boulder. Speakers include writers, Dr Carl Sagan, Luisa Valenzuela, Rigoberta Menchu, William Styron, William Gass, Robert Coover and Peter Mathiessen; politicians, Dr Oscar Arias, former president of Costa Rica, Cuauhtemoc Cardenas of Mexico; Nobel Peace Prize Winner Alberto Perez Esquivel of Argentina and surprise guest Salman Rushdie. Commenting on the massive security presence at the venue, Mr Rushdie says: "The government of Iran is obliging a major security operation to take place in the United States without lifting a finger. Unfortunately this appears to be the first instance of an entirely new form of international terrorism. When those forms seem to be working, they get repeated." The author says that Iranian authors have been put to death and others imprisoned for their work: "ten or eleven Iranian writers have disappeared", adding that they are probably buried in unmarked graves.

30 September 1992: Day 1324
The Frankfurt Book Fair opens with a continued ban on participation by Iranian publishers until the *fatwa* against

Salman Rushdie and those associated with publication of *The Satanic Verses* is revoked.

13 October 1992: Day 1337
In Helsinki, Salman Rushdie addresses the Nordic Council's International Conference on Culture, which is attended by senior politicians from all the Nordic countries as well as from Belgium, Estonia, Germany, Latvia, Lithuania, Poland, Portugal, Russia and Switzerland. His speech refers to Milan Kundera's recent essay, *Europe – Culture of the Novel*, and he describes the condemnation of *The Satanic Verses* by people who had not read it: "It took me by surprise that a book could be so falsely described. What a sadness that this novel is condemned unread. Perhaps this is what always happens when people condemn novels. This is a moment of truth. Will the culture of the novel be able to defend itself?" Referring to the Iranian government's accusation that Western culture has no values or belief systems, the author says: "It's very important to show that this culture, the culture of freedom, does have values. There are principles that will be defended with equal conviction."

15 October 1992: Day 1339
Norwegian political leaders, authors, publishers, representatives of writers', editors' and translators' unions launch the Norwegian Support Committee for Salman Rushdie.

25 October 1992: Day 1349
Salman Rushdie and members of the Rushdie Defence Committee visit Bonn, Germany, to meet with senior politicians, and are welcomed by the President of German PEN and Dr Friedbert Pflüger of the Christian Democrat Party.

26 October 1992: Day 1350
Salman Rushdie meets with the Chairman of the SPD, who promises that his party will formally support Rushdie.

27 October 1992: Day 1351
Salman Rushdie meets with Dr Schirmer, Head of the

Cultural Directory within the German Foreign Ministry.

28 October 1992: Day 1352
Salman Rushdie meets with the President of the German Parliament, Frau Prof Dr Rita Süssmuth, and Dr Rutgers of the Foreign Relations Committee. Separate meetings are held with other politicians.

At the initiative of Tahar Ben Jelloun, Paris-based Morrocan writer and novelist, a petition is sent to UNESCO Director-General Federico Mayor, calling on him to intervene on Salman Rushdie's behalf during his forthcoming visit to Tehran.

30 October 1992: Day 1354
The Iranian Embassy in Bonn issues a statement which speaks out against confusing the "judgement on apostasy" against Rushdie with the conduct of the Iranian government in the field of international affairs.

2 November 1992: Day 1357
The Iranian Ambassador to Bonn reacts angrily to German politicians meeting with Salman Rushdie. He is summoned to the Foreign Ministry and told that the position of the Federal government is quite clear: it will protect Salman Rushdie; it condemns the *fatwa*; demands that the Iranian government work towards rescinding the death threat; and states that it is time for the Iranian government to make its position publicly known.

Hassani Sanei, head of the 15 Khordad Foundation, increases the bounty money on Salman Rushdie's life to include "material and political help", because of the author's visit to Germany.

A UK Foreign Office spokesman says: "The bounty on Mr Rushdie's head has always been a monstrosity. We consider the Iranian death threat to be an unacceptable infringement of his rights as a British citizen."

4 November 1992: Day 1359
In the House of Commons, an Early Day Motion supported

by more than 100 MPs condemns the increase in bounty money and demands that "the Prime Minister, as President of the EC, does all that he can together with our EC partners to end the *fatwa* and protect Mr Rushdie's civil rights".

5 November 1992: Day 1360
Salman Rushdie arrives in Sweden where he addresses the Swedish Academy. He points out that what, in his opinion, had angered the Iranian government is the fact that *The Satanic Verses* is about good and evil existing within a person and not without. Part of his intention, he says, was to reflect in his books the joy of the East and to translate that to Western cultures. He ends by saying that if this campaigns fails, it will be an ominous and tragic signal to persecuted writers the world over, particularly in Islamic countries.

6 November 1992: 1361
Salman Rushdie is awarded the Kurt Tucholsky Prize – given to writers in exile – by Deputy Prime Minister Bengt Westerberg, who pledges his government's support for Mr Rushdie as an individual and also for the fundamental right to freedom of expression.

Salman Rushdie meets with the former Prime Minister and leader of the Social Democratic Party, the Minister of Education, the Prime Minister's advisor, leading publishers, and many Swedish writers, artists, journalists and critics.

10 November 1992: Day 1365
In Iran, Chief Justice Morteza Moqtadaei states that Muslims are obliged to kill Salman Rushdie for his alleged blasphemies against Islam in his novel *The Satanic Verses*.

11 November 1992: Day 1366
In Tehran, Hassani Sanei, head of the 15 Khordad Foundation, says that volunteer hit squads are to be despatched to kill Salman Rushdie.

At Aarhus, Denmark, foreign ministers from the five Nordic countries announce: "We will summon Iran's diplomatic representatives to our Foreign Ministries to express

our deep concern about the so-called death sentence on
Salman Rushdie."

12 November 1992: Day 1367
The Iranian Chargé d'Affaires in London is summoned to
the Foreign Office to receive an official protest at the
renewed demands for the death sentence to be carried out
on Salman Rushdie.

17 November 1992: Day 1372
Salman Rushdie remains in deep hiding, under armed
guard.

About the authors

Margaret Atwood. Born in Ottawa in 1939, she is Canada's most eminent novelist, poet and critic. Her first volume of poetry, *The Circle Game* (1966), won the Governor-General's Award. Since then she has published fourteen volumes of poetry and a study of Canadian literature, *Survival*. Her first novel, *The Edible Woman*, was published in 1969, followed by *Surfacing, Lady Oracle, Life Before Man, Bodily Harm* and *The Handmaid's Tale*, winner of the Arthur C. Clarke Award and shortlisted for the Booker Prize. She has published three collections of short stories, *Dancing Girls, Bluebeard's Egg* and *Wilderness Tips*. *Cat's Eye*, published in 1989, was also shortlisted for the Booker Prize.

Dermot Bolger. Born in Finglas, North Dublin, in 1959, his first two novels of Dublin life, *Night Shift* and *The Woman's Daughter*, have received the AE Memorial Award, the Macaulay Fellowship and the *Sunday Tribune* Arts Award. *The Journey Home* was published to critical acclaim in 1990, *Emily's Shoes* in 1992. The author of five collections of poetry, his first play, *The Lament for Arthur Cleary*, received the Samuel Beckett Award and the Stewart Parker BBC Award. His other plays include *In High Germany, The Holy Ground* and *One Last White Horse*.

Peter Carey. Born in Bacchus Marsh, Victoria, in 1943, he worked as an advertizing copywriter, then left Australia for a while to live in London. His first book was a collection of short stories, *The Fat Man in History* (1974). He explored the world of advertizing in *Bliss* (1981), and in 1985 *Illywhacker* was nominated for the Booker Prize. In 1988 he won the Booker Prize with *Oscar and Lucinda*. His fourth novel, *The Tax Inspector*, was published in 1991.

Fahimeh Farsaie. Born in 1952 in Tehran, where from 1971 to 1976 she studied law and history of art. In 1972 she was detained for having written a short story critical of the regime and spent 18 months in jail. Then she worked as a sub-editor for a daily paper, was sacked by the Khomeini regime in 1982, and fled to West Berlin in 1983. In Germany she published a book of short stories, *The Glass Home Country* (1989), and the novel *Poisoned Time – The Case of Dr Danesh* (1991).

Ralph Giordano. Born in Hamburg in 1923, the son of a Jewish mother, he survived Hitler's Germany in hiding. Since 1945 he has worked as a journalist, writer and author of TV documentaries. He became known to a wider audience through his novel and television film, *The Bertinis*. In 1989 he published *Israel, for Heaven's Sake, Israel*.

Nadine Gordimer. Born in 1923 in Springs, Transvaal, her work is rooted in South Africa and has as a constant theme the racial bigotry of an apartheid society. Many of her books have been banned in South Africa. She published two books of short stories before her first novel, *The Lying Days* (1953). In 1974 her novel, *The Conversationist*, was joint winner of the Booker Prize. She has also been awarded the Malaparte Prize (Italy), the Nelly Sachs Prize (Germany), the Grand Aigle d'Or (France), the Neil Gunn Fellowship (Scotland), and in 1991 she won the Nobel Prize for Literature.

Günter Grass. Born in Danzig (Gdansk) in 1927, he trained as a stonemason and sculptor. He served in World War II, lived for a time after the war in Paris, and was a speechwriter for Willy Brandt when he was mayor of West Berlin. His first novel, *The Tin Drum* (1962; originally *Die Blechtrommel*, 1959), quickly established him as one of Germany's foremost novelists. He is also a playwright and poet, and some of his principal works are *Cat and Mouse* (1963; *Katz und Maus*, 1961), *Dog Years* (1965; *Hundejahre*, 1963) and *The Flounder* (1978; *Der Butt*, 1977). His latest novel, *The Call of the Toad*, was published in spring of 1992.

Pierre Guyotat. Born in Bourg-Argental in 1940 he worked for the *Nouvel Observateur* in the sixties. His first novel, *Sur un Cheval*, was published by Gallimard in 1961. His prolific output includes *Ashby* (1964), *Tombeau pour cinq cent mille Soldats* (1967), *Eden, Eden, Eden* (1970), *Littérature Interdite* (1972), *Prostitution* (1975), *Le Livre: Vivre* (1984) and *Denoël* (1984). He has also written a stage play, *Bivouac* (1987).

Kazuo Ishiguro. Born in Nagasaki, Japan, in 1954 and came to Britain in 1960. He attended the University of Kent at Canterbury and the University of East Anglia. He now lives in London. His first novel, *A Pale View of Hills* (1982), was awarded the Winifred Holtby Prize by the Royal Society of Literature and has been translated into thirteen languages. His second novel, *An Artist of the Floating World* (1986), was shortlisted for the Booker Prize and won the Whitbread Book of the Year award for 1986; it has been translated into fourteen languages. His third novel, *The Remains of the Day*, was published in 1990; shortlisted for the Booker, it is about to be made into a film. Kazuo Ishiguro is also the author of two original screenplays for Channel 4 Television: *A Profile of Arthur J. Mason* and *The Gourmet*.

Elfriede Jelinek. Born in Styria in 1946, Elfriede Jelinek lives in Vienna and Munich. She has written several novels – *Wonderful, Wonderful Times, The Piano Teacher, Lust* – as well as radio and television plays.

Lev Kopalev. Born in Kiev in 1912, he worked as a journalist before studying philosophy in Moscow. He was a propaganda officer during the war but fell foul of the authorities and was sentenced to ten years penal servitude. Rehabilitated in 1956, he worked in Moscow until 1968 when he was dismissed for sympathizing with dissidents and expelled from the party. In 1981 while on a visit to West Germany his Soviet citizenship was revoked. From 1982 he taught at Wüppertal University and is the recipient of the prestigious German Booksellers Peace Prize. He has published many scholarly monographs on philosophy and literature.

Mario Vargas Llosa. Born in Arequipa, Peru, in 1936, he is a former President of PEN (1976-79) and he has won many awards, including the Ritz Paris Hemingway award. A thousand copies of his first, satirical novel, *The Time of the Hero* (1962), were publicly burned. Since then he has become one of the world's great novelists, among whose works are *The Green House* (1965), *Conversation in the Cathedral* (1969), *Aunt Julia and the Scriptwriter* (1977), *The War at the End of the World* (1981) and *Who Killed Palomino Molero?* (1987). He declined the offer of the Peruvian premiership in 1984 but was subsequently a candidate for the presidency. He is also a football commentator.

Norman Mailer. Born in 1923 in Long Branch, New Jersey, he was brought up in Brooklyn and educated at Harvard. His first novel, *The Naked and the Dead* (1948), draws on his World War II experience. He became a proponent of the New Journalism, a social critic, a polemicist and a protester. *Advertisements for Myself* (1959), *An American Dream* (1965) and *Why Are We in Vietnam?* (1967) were some of his earlier books, and in 1968 he won the National Book Award and the Pulitzer Prize for *Armies of the Night*. Other titles in his enormous body of work include *Miami and the Siege of Chicago* (1969), *The Prisoner of Sex* (1971), *Marilyn* (1973), *The Executioner's Song* (1979), *Ancient Evenings* (1983) and *Tough Guys Don't Dance* (1984). In 1992 his gargantuan epic novel, *Harlot's Ghost*, was published.

Salman Rushdie. Born in Bombay in June 1947. His grandfather was an Urdu poet, his father a student of Arabic, Persian and Western literature and his mother had a genius for family history. He was educated at Rugby and King's College, Cambridge, where he read History and was a member of Footlights. After graduating he returned to his family who had moved to Pakistan. He wrote for television but, feeling his talents were being wasted, he went back to England.

During the 1970s he worked in advertising and wrote his first published novel, *Grimus*, a fantasy. This was followed in 1981 by *Midnight's Children*, which won the Booker Prize, the James Tait Black Memorial Prize, an Arts Council Literary Bursary and the American English Speaking Union Literary Award. His next novel, *Shame* (1983), was shortlisted for the Booker Prize. In *The Satanic Verses* (1989) he turned his imaginative attention to Islam. He has also written an award-winning children's book, *Haroun and the Sea of Stories* (1991).

José Saramago. Born in Azinhaga in 1922, he is one of the most important contemporary novelists in Portugal. With his novel *The Gospel According to Jesus Christ*, published in Portugal and Brazil in 1991, he provoked intense debate about the role of religion and the church. Other novels are *Balthasar and Blimuda* and the *Year of the Death of Ricardo Reis*.

Johannes Mario Simmel. Born in 1924 in Vienna, he is one of the most successful novelists in the German language, with book sales of 65 million to his credit. He is best known for his novel, *It Doesn't Always Have to be Caviar* (1960).

Gertrud Seehaus. Born in 1934, she worked for twelve years as a teacher and then lived for a number of years in Jerusalem. She began to write only when she was in her forties. A member of German PEN she lives in Cologne; her most recent novel is *Regards to Ivan B.*

Tom Stoppard. Born in Zlin, Czechoslovakia, in 1937, his family settled in Bristol, England, in 1946, where he became a journalist; in 1960 he moved to London where he worked as a journalist and theatre critic. His first play, *A Walker on the Water* (1960), was followed by radio plays, including *The Dissolution of Dominic Boot* (1964), and he came to prominence with *Rosencrantz and Guildenstern Are Dead* (1967), which transferred from the Edinburgh Festival to the National Theatre and won the *Evening Standard* Award. Other plays include *The Real Inspector Hound* (1968), *Jumpers* (1972), *Travesties* (1974) and *Professional Foul* (1977). He has also written a novel, short stories, screenplays and film scripts.

William Styron. Born in Newport News, Virginia, in 1925, his first novel, *Lie Down in Darkness*, was published in 1951. His novel about racism, *The Confessions of Nat Turner*, won him the Pulitzer Prize in 1967. Another novel, *Sophie's Choice*, dealt with the Holocaust and its effects on those who survived it (1979). He has also written *Set This House on Fire* and *The Long March*.

Graham Swift. Born in London in 1949. He was nominated as one of the twenty Best of Young British Novelists in the Book Marketing Council's promotion in 1983. His first novel, *The Sweet Shop Owner*, was published in 1980. *Shuttlecock*, his second novel, was published in 1981 and was awarded the bi-annual Geoffrey Faber Memorial Prize in 1983. A collection of short stories, *Learning to Swim*, appeared in 1982. In 1983 *Waterland* was published and was shortlisted for the Booker Prize in that year. His most recent novels are *Out of this World* (1988) and *Ever After* (1992).

Andrzej Szczypiorski. Born in Warsaw in 1924, he took part in the Warsaw Rising and was interned in Sachsenhausen concentration camp. After the war he worked as a diplomat and journalist; he served as a member of the Polish Senate from 1989 to 1991. His work includes the novels *Beautiful Mrs Seidenman* and *Night, Day and Night*, and a collection of short stories, *Amerikan Whiskey*.

Paul Theroux. Born in 1941 in Medford, Massachusetts. His first novel, *Waldo*, was published in 1967, and other novels drew on time spent in Africa. He moved to Singapore, which provided the setting for a collection of short stories and a novel. He has lived in London in recent years, and his other novels include *Picture Palace* (1978), which won the Whitbread Literary Award, *The Mosquito Coast* (*Yorkshire Post* Novel of the Year, 1981) and *The London Embassy* (1982). But he is probably best known for his development of a new type of travel writing, in books such as *The Great Railway Bazaar: By Train Through Asia* (1975), *The Old Patagonian Express: By Train Through the Americas* (1979) and *Riding the Iron Rooster* (1988).

Dragan Velikic. Born in Belgrade in 1953, he has published two collections of short stories and two novels. In 1983 he received the respected Yugoslav Milos Crnjanski Prize for *Via Fula*. Velikic has also published essays on, among others, Peter Handke, Elias Canetti and Claudio Magris.

Jatinder Verma. Born in Dar es Salaam of Indian parents in 1954, he emigrated to Britain in 1968. After the "racialist summer" of 1976 he founded Tara Arts Group, which created an innovative

Anglo-Asian theatrical style. The Rushdie affair led him to write a new adaption of Molière's *Tartuffe.*

Joachim Walther. Born in 1943 in Chemnitz, he worked as a publisher's reader with Verlag Der Morgen until 1983 when he was forced to resign. In 1990 he became Vice-President of the Writers' Union of the then German Democratic Republic. He has written novels, radio plays, short stories and children's books.

Arnold Wesker. Born in the East End of London in 1932, of a Russian-Hungarian-Jewish background, he came to immediate attention as a dramatist with his first play, *The Kitchen* (1959), which was quickly followed with the trilogy, *Chicken Soup with Barley, Roots* and *I'm talking about Jerusalem* (1959-60). In 1961 he played a leading role in the Committee of 100's demonstrations against the use of nuclear weapons and, together with Bertrand Russell and others, was sentenced to a month in prison. He also became a director of Centre 42, a cultural movement for popularizing the arts. One of the foremost playwrights of the 1960s, his other plays include *Chips With Everything* (1962), *The Four Seasons* (1966), *The Old Ones* (1972) and *The Merchant* (1978).

Avraham B. Yehoshua. Born in Jerusalem in 1936, he is one of Israel's best-known novelists; his collection of short stories, *Continuing Silence of the Poet* (1968), has a special place in modern Israeli prose. His successful 1980 novel, *Five Seasons,* concerned the Arab-Israeli conflict, a theme which informs much of Yehoshua's writing; a further novel, *Mr Manni,* was published in 1991. He teaches at the University of Haifa.

Organizations constituting the International Committee for the Defence of Salman Rushdie and his Publishers (UK) include:

Article 19, Arts Council of Great Britain, Association of Authors' Agents, Association of Cinematograph Television and allied Technicians, Black Voices in Support of Salman Rushdie and *The Satanic Verses* Book Trust, Booksellers Association of Great Britain and Ireland, Charter 88, English Centre of International PEN, Independent Publishers Guild, Index on Censorship, International Booksellers' Federation, International Press Institute, Islington Friends of Salman Rushdie, Library Association, National Council for Civil Liberties, National Union of Journalists, New Statesman and Society, Poets International, Publishers Association, Rationalist Press Association, Society of Authors, Tara Arts Group/Black Theatre Forum, Theatre Writers' Union, Writers Guild of Great Britain

The Committee acts in liaison with over 120 writers' groups in more than 40 countries worldwide. Special thanks to the following supporting groups for their contributions to this chronology:

American Civil Liberties Union, American PEN Centre, Anti-Censorship Action Group (South Africa), Article 19 (USA), Association of American Publishers, British Humanist Association, Byelorussian PEN Centre, Canadian PEN Centre (International PEN), Congress of South African Writers, Danish PEN Centre, Fellowship of Australian Writers, Free Speech Committee (Australia), Fund for Free Expression, German PEN Centre, Hong Kong Journalists' Association, Human Rights Watch, International Federation of Journalists, Irish Translators' Association, Irish Writers' Union, Kurdish PEN Centre, La Ligue des droits de l'homme (France), National Secular Society (UK), National Union of Journalists (Ireland), National Writers' Union, New Zealand PEN Centre, Norwegian Association of Literary Translators, Norwegian Authors' Union, Norwegian Newspaper Editors' Association, Norwegian PEN Club, Norwegian Playwrights Guild, Norwegian Publishers' Association, Norwegian Union of Journalists, Norwegian Writers' Union, Peace Pledge Union (UK), Reporters sans Frontières (France), Society of Irish Playwrights, South Place Ethical Society, Swedish PEN Centre, Swedish Writers' Union.